NEW HORIZONS IN CRIMINOLOGY

WILDLIFE CRIMINOLOGY

Angus Nurse and Tanya Wyatt

BRISTOL
UNIVERSITY
PRESS

New Horizons in Criminology series

Series editor: **Andrew Millie**, Edge Hill University, UK

New Horizons in Criminology series provides concise, authoritative texts which reflect cutting-edge thought and theoretical development with an international scope. Written by leading authors in their fields, the series has become essential reading for all academics and students interested in where criminology is heading.

Forthcoming in the series:

Transnational Criminology
Trafficking and Global Criminal Markets
Simon Mackenzie, September 2021

Out now in the series:

Imaginative Criminology
Of Spaces Past, Present and Future
Maggie O'Neill and **Lizzie Seal**, July 2019

A Criminology of War?
Ross McGarry and **Sandra Walklate**, July 2019

A Criminology of Policing and Security Frontiers
Randy Lippert and **Kevin Walby**, February 2019

A Criminology of Moral Order
Hans Boutellier, January 2019

Climate Change Criminology
Rob White, October 2018

Find out more at

bristoluniversitypress.co.uk/new-horizons-in-criminology

Thank you to all our colleagues, friends and family –
two- and four-legged – for your support and inspiration

First published in Great Britain in 2021 by

Bristol University Press
University of Bristol
1-9 Old Park Hill
Bristol
BS2 8BB
UK
t: +44 (0)117 954 5940
e: bup-info@bristol.ac.uk

Details of international sales and distribution partners are available at bristoluniversitypress.co.uk

© Bristol University Press 2021

British Library Cataloguing in Publication Data
A catalogue record for this book is available from the British Library

ISBN 978-1-5292-0439-1 paperback
ISBN 978-1-5292-0434-6 hardcover
ISBN 978-1-5292-0436-0 ePub
ISBN 978-1-5292-0435-3 ePdf

Cover design: Bristol University Press
Front cover image: Getty Images

Contents

About the Authors

Angus Nurse joined Middlesex University in May 2013. Previously he was Lecturer in Criminology at Birmingham City University, and Research Fellow in the Law School at the University of Lincoln before that. Angus's main research interests are in wildlife and environmental crime and the effectiveness of laws protecting animals and wildlife. His work in this area includes examining the links between animal abuse and interpersonal violence, the use of justice systems to achieve better protection for animals and to pursue animal rights and the better integration of wildlife crime within mainstream criminal justice.

Tanya Wyatt joined Northumbria University in October 2010. She was previously a United States Peace Corps volunteer in Ukraine and a police officer for nearly five years in the US. Tanya's main research interests are in non-human animal abuse and wildlife crime and trafficking. Her work in these areas has focused on the intersections of organised and corporate crime as well as the role of corruption.

NEW HORIZONS IN CRIMINOLOGY

Series editor: Professor Andrew Millie, Department of Law and Criminology, Edge Hill University, UK

Preface

The aim of the New Horizons in Criminology series is to provide high-quality and authoritative texts that reflect cutting-edge thought and theoretical development in criminology, have an international scope and are also accessible and concise. This book certainly fits that brief. *Wildlife Criminology* is a much-needed and timely contribution to the literature and, having built quite a reputation in this area, Angus Nurse and Tanya Wyatt were the right people to write it. Writing alone or together, or with others, Angus and Tanya have authored some key texts on wildlife crime and on green criminology more broadly (for example, Nurse, 2013, 2015, 2016; Wyatt, 2013; Hall et al, 2017). The current text is the logical culmination of much of this work and proposes a specific 'wildlife criminology'.

The book opens with the observation that 'The harm and crime committed by humans does not only affect humans.' This is such a simple statement, yet it is a fundamental challenge to the anthropocentrism of criminology. The response is, well, what can we do – or ought we do – about this? And is it a criminological concern? After reading this book the reader is left with little doubt that wildlife *is* of criminological interest. The authors clearly unpack what they mean by harm and crime to non-human species and 'develop criminological thinking in respect of the importance of non-human animals within law and order discourse' (p 2). Their focus is on both crime *and* harm, because much that humans do to animals is harmful, yet is not necessarily a breach of criminal law.

The book is concerned with animal wildlife while recognising that wildlife encompasses other forms of life as well. As highlighted in the book's conclusions, non-animal wildlife will be an important consideration for the future of wildlife criminology. Angus and Tanya examine the commodification and exploitation of wildlife in the context that much wildlife is perceived as human property there for human consumption as food, sport or entertainment. Our response to this may be to protect; yet the authors highlight that wildlife protection and classification can also reflect speciesism, with a social construction of wildlife that is 'deserving' or 'undeserving' of protection – a narrative of victimhood that will be familiar to many criminologists and victimologists. Drawing on Tanya's earlier work in this area (Wyatt, 2013), the authors note a 'hierarchy of victimhood [where] [c]harismatic megafauna are the species most worthy of human attention and protection' (p 14). It is much harder to garner enthusiasm for wildlife that is less exciting. This, the authors say, is a form of 'othering'.

Angus and Tanya also explore violence and wildlife. For instance, we can be fascinated by violence among animals. For the authors this translates into an evolutionary interpretation of human violence – that to act violently is to behave like an animal. The authors counter this by demonstrating altruism among some non-human species. Links between human violence and animal abuse are then explored. The authors also consider the possibility of rights for animals and for wider wildlife.

Angus Nurse and Tanya Wyatt deserve much praise for this little book. They clearly position wildlife criminology within broader green criminology, and there are aspects of their writing that are of interest to climate change criminology (for example, White, 2018). Yet they have identified a highly important *new horizon* for criminology. When I first envisioned the New Horizons in Criminology book series, this is precisely what I was after. I believe there is much here that will interest the green criminologist, but also criminologists with interests that are not traditionally regarded as 'green'. It ought to be required reading for other academics and practitioners in the wildlife and conservation industries as well.

References

Hall, M., Wyatt, T., South, N., Nurse, A., Potter, G. and Maher, J. (eds) (2017) *Greening criminology in the 21st century: Contemporary debates and future directions in the study of environmental harm.* Abingdon: Routledge

Nurse, A. (2013) *Animal harm: Perspectives on why people kill and harm animals.* Farnham: Ashgate

Nurse, A. (2015) *Policing wildlife: Perspectives on the enforcement of wildlife legislation.* London: Palgrave Macmillan

Nurse, A. (2016) *An introduction to green criminology and environmental justice,* London: Sage

White, R. (2018) *Climate change criminology.* Bristol: Bristol University Press

Wyatt, T. (2013) *Wildlife trafficking: A deconstruction of the crime, the victims and the offenders.* Basingstoke: Palgrave Macmillan

1

Introduction:
Wildlife and Criminology

The harm and crime committed by humans does not only affect humans. Victimisation is not isolated to people, but instead encompasses the planet and other beings. Yet apart from fairly recent green criminological scholarship employing an expanded criminological gaze beyond the human, the discipline of criminology has largely confined itself to human victims, ignoring the human-caused suffering and plight of the billions of other individuals with whom we share the Earth. This book tries to take a further step in rectifying criminology's blindness to the non-human world and in advancing scholarly discourse on social harm (Hillyard and Tombs, 2007). In order take this step, we propose a 'wildlife criminology'. From the outset, we make clear that in choosing the term 'wildlife criminology' our intention is not to create a new and distinct subfield of criminology. To do so would suggest that we do not consider green criminology to be adequate or sustainable as an academic endeavour – something that neither of us believes. The goal is to create a complementary project that expands the existing green and critical criminological scholarship even further beyond that of the human.

As the book's chapters will demonstrate, criminology's current and future engagement with wildlife issues needs to develop by considering wider notions of crime and harm involving non-human animals and plants, and this argument is developed in respect of both mainstream and green criminology. Criminological discourse has somewhat engaged with issues around wildlife trafficking and non-human animal abuse (Wellsmith, 2011; Nurse, 2013; Wyatt, 2013a; Beirne, 2018; Sollund, 2019) and at the time of writing this book wildlife trafficking is a hot topic, attracting both scholarly attention and some grant funding. However, we contend that a limited notion of wildlife crime currently exists and is perpetuated in criminological and political discourse. Wildlife crime is frequently reduced to discussion of trafficking in non-human animals and wildlife derivatives with wider conceptions, implications and the importance of wildlife crime often neglected.

As the first foray into wildlife criminology, this book explores how criminology deals with crimes against and involving non-human animals, and examines the failure of criminology and justice systems to deal with non-human animals as victims of crime and wider social harm. Pemberton (2016: xi–xii) commented on the need for criminology to 'encompass a typology of social harms, irrespective of legal categorisation' and to engage with the concept of zemiology, a social harm-based approach to crime and justice. In part, this book does so, in particular by exploring wildlife as victims and participants in crime and social harm underpinned by four themes: commodification and exploitation, violence, rights, and speciesism and 'othering'. These themes feature in each of the chapters to varying degrees, but are present throughout our discussion. Our aim is, in part, to develop criminological thinking in respect of the importance of non-human animals within law and order discourse. In doing so, we draw on our shared experience of examining and writing about crimes against, and of investigating harms inflicted on, non-human animals. Often such harms reveal wider social ills or are indicative of other forms of deviance. Yet too often, the policy or policing response asserts the anthropocentric viewpoint that 'it's just an animal'. Our contention is that harm and deviance directed at non-human animals are of importance because of and beyond the direct harm caused to the non-human animal. In this respect, we draw on the zemiological principle that what matters is the harm caused (in this case to wildlife) rather than whether that harm is classed by legal systems as 'crime'. However, in keeping with green criminological perspectives that argue for dedicated attention to green crimes and harms (Lynch and Stretesky, 2014; White and Heckenberg, 2014), we argue that the scale and nature of harms against wildlife are worthy of distinct inquiry. Rather than being considered as part of a general approach to social harm, wildlife harms are worthy of distinct attention within a wider social harm discourse. We propose this is the case because such harms are committed against sentient beings, who fall outside the mainstream of social harm considerations and who are classified by most legal systems as being distinctly 'other'. Despite long running advocacy for the rights of non-human animals (Singer, [1975] 1990; Wise, 2000, 2013), they remain outside the scope of human rights and thus their concerns are marginalised in policy, legal protection and social harm discourse.

Whereas our focus in this first book is on non-human animals, we recognise that wildlife also includes plants and fungi, and the immense diversity within those kingdoms. Our intention is not to perpetuate the 'plant blindness' inherent in criminology and policy, but to pave the way for expanded discussions of victimhood and harm by first exposing the shortcomings related to wild non-human animals. We hope our wildlife criminology project will inspire others to speak out for the range of other beings affected by human exploitation. To begin, we first set out our conceptualisation of wildlife before detailing the need for a wildlife criminology and the themes that underpin it.

Wildlife, humans and justice

In setting out our case for a wildlife criminology within (green) criminological discourse and developing the wildlife criminology concept, this book examines the various ways in which crime and justice discourse defines wildlife for the purposes of legal protection and in policy debates. It also sets out our arguments for the need for a wildlife criminology, noting that wildlife-related crime and harm are significant issues within crime and justice discourse, and there is often a link between wildlife crimes and other offending. However, currently, criminology and legal discourse lacks a common definition of wildlife and wildlife crime, and thus also lacks a consensus on the importance of harms visited on wildlife.

What is wildlife?

At its most basic level, wildlife is defined as the native fauna and flora of a state and is arguably commonly understood to mean animals that live in a wild state outside human control. US professor of animal law Joan Schaffner (2011: 59) identifies that one US federal conservation statute defines wildlife as 'any wild animal ... including without limitation any wild mammal, bird, reptile, amphibian, fish, mollusc, crustacean, arthropod, coelenterate, or other invertebrate, whether or not bred, hatched, or born in captivity', thus covering a wide range of vertebrate and invertebrate species. This definition also includes 'any part, product, egg or offspring thereof' (Schaffner, 2011: 59), providing a definition that includes non-human animals alive or dead, those yet to be born, and the products derived from once living wildlife (for example, shawls made from skins and knife handles and other carvings made from bone). This definition is, however, confined to non-human animal species (for example, those beings currently existing in a wild state or recognised as having existed in the wild), whereas a definition of wildlife that includes plants is deployed within the Convention on International Trade in Endangered Species of Wild Fauna and Flora (CITES), the international legislation that regulates the trade in wildlife. Similarly, wildlife crime definitions sometimes include fish and plants within definitions of wildlife, but sometimes do not. Accordingly, definitions of wildlife are socially constructed and a uniform discussion of what constitutes 'wildlife' is problematic within criminological discourse.

Wyatt (2013a: 2) defines wildlife as 'taken to comprise all non-human animals and plants that are not companion animals or domesticated animals', which incorporates plants and trees as well as arguably non-domesticated farmed animals. Nurse (2015: 27) defines wildlife as 'wild birds, animals, reptiles, fish, mammals, plants or trees which form part of a country's natural environment or which are visitors in a wild state'. Both authors of this book thus consider that the definition of wildlife appropriate to criminological consideration of wildlife harms needs to consider both non-human animals and plants that are the subjects of anthropocentric exploitation and destruction. Wildlife in our wildlife criminology project is therefore defined as *all non-human animals, plants and fungi which form part of a country's natural environment or which are visitors in a wild or captured state*. We, too, like Beirne (2018), are not completely at ease with this definition, since the metric for wildlife is in reference to not being human, which perpetuates the anthropocentrism we are trying to challenge. The phrase 'non-human animal', while used throughout this book, serves as an inadequate shorthand for tens of thousands of species.

Our definition excludes companion animals and domesticated animals but not because the harms visited against them are any less. Indeed, non-human animal cruelty figures produced by the various animal welfare protection and investigation agencies such as the American Society for the Prevention of Cruelty to Animals (ASPCA) and the UK's Royal Society for the Prevention of Cruelty to Animals (RSPCA) routinely show high levels of crimes against companion animals. Investigations by bodies such as the International Fund for Animal Welfare (IFAW) and People for the Ethical Treatment of Animals (PETA) also show animal cruelty offences committed in respect of non-human animals in the community and in farming and exploitation practices such as the leather industry (PETA, 2018). However, while such non-human animal suffering is serious and seemingly widespread, the focus of our inquiry is not on companion animal welfare and regulatory offences committed against non-human animals that are in one sense routinely under human control. Arguably, many such offences already fall within the remit of criminological consideration where, for example, there is a link between the harm visited on non-human animals and human violence such as the link between companion animal abuse and subsequent human violence (Linzey, 2009; Nurse, 2013). Non-human animal abuse that clearly involves violent acts and the death of a non-human animal might also draw criminological attention where firearms or torture are involved as these arguably fall within criminological consideration of deviance, non-conformity and violence (Schneider, 2008). Criminological consideration is also possible where corruption or fraud in an industry draws the attention of legal and socio-legal scholars or criminologists; for example, corruption in horse racing (Brooks et al, 2013), which can be associated with fraud and illegal gambling that are mainstream criminological concerns. While we acknowledge these anthropocentric non-human animal harms, our focus is on those wildlife not *routinely* under human control, which is why non-domesticated non-human animals in captivity (such as zoos and so forth) are included in our explorations.

What is wildlife crime?

Examination of wildlife criminology also requires consideration of legal and socially constructed notions of non-human animal protection. The reality of most legal systems, as we discuss later in this chapter and in Chapter 2, is that non-human animals have the status of human property (Schaffner, 2011: 5). Sometimes, they are protected from a range of harmful actions and cruel practices, though wildlife can generally be killed and exploited for human benefit, subject to various conditions. Thus 'animal legislation serves multiple purposes and is intended to address a variety of human activities considered harmful towards animals, although arguably animal law is primarily aimed at preserving human interests' (Nurse, 2013: 6). Accordingly, non-human animals are generally only protected to the extent that doing so provides some form of human benefit, whether economic or otherwise. As such, the nature and extent of wildlife 'crime' – here in the strictest sense of the word of crime that only includes actions prohibited by criminal statutes – is limited. Legislation recognising that wildlife should be protected for its intrinsic value, because wild animals are sentient beings deserving to live a life free of suffering (Wise, 2000) and because protection of wildlife and maintaining good standards of non-human animal welfare represent a public good (Nurse, 2016b), is mostly non-existent. Wildlife protection legislation is limited by the fundamental principle that such laws operate primarily on the basis of the sustainable use of wildlife. Thus, while offences are created by wildlife protection laws and various methods of taking or harming wildlife can be explicitly prohibited by law, the underlying principle remains one of allowing the use and consumption of wildlife.

This means that a vast majority of the harm and suffering of wildlife is legal. Donaldson and Kymlicka (2011: 156–7) in their political science theory *Zoopolis*, identify that some of the harms visited on wildlife include

> direct, intentional violence such as hunting, fishing and trapping; the kidnapping of animals from the wild in order to stock zoos and circuses, or to meet demand for exotic pet-keeping and trophy-collecting, or other wild animal body or body part uses; the killing of animals as part of wildlife management programmes; and harmful experimentation on wild animals in the name of scientific research.

To reiterate, all of what is outlined here by Donaldson and Kymlicka are not considered to be crimes. For these actions to be criminal there would need to be specific prohibition making the killing, taking, trading and/or sale of wildlife *illegal* by the legal systems and subject to some form of criminal sanction. However, there is a legal trade in non-human animals and most countries recognise hunting and fishing as sports that are legal subject to regulations such as limits on what can be killed or taken. Hunting and game laws often also specify regulated seasons dictating when non-human animals or fish can be killed or taken and when they are otherwise protected. In addition, the killing of wildlife as part of wildlife management or conservation programmes is most likely legal when conducted in accordance with the provisions of any such approved programme. Although hotly disputed by non-human animal rights activists and non-human animal protection advocates, killing of 'surplus' animals is a recognised wildlife management technique that may be sanctioned by governments as a means of providing for 'efficient' management of wild animals (Lacy, 1995; Chee and Wintle, 2010). Similarly, although controversial and continually opposed by animal protection bodies like PETA and Cruelty Free International (formerly BUAV, the British Union for the Abolition of Vivisection), experimentation on non-human animals can be legal when conducted in accordance with relevant regulations, such as the UK's Animals (Scientific Procedures) Act 1986 and any licences issued under the regulations.

As these examples show, defining wildlife crime requires some consideration of the difficulty in distinguishing between when the law allows wildlife to be killed and taken and when non-human animals are taken in contravention of these laws. Criminology's historic focus on wildlife trafficking makes sense because trafficking by its very nature involves illegal acts that are the core focus of criminology (Edwards and Gill, 2004). However, our discussion of wildlife crime expands beyond the traditional analysis of wildlife trafficking that is a mainstay of criminological wildlife debate. We consider a somewhat broader notion of wildlife crime as part of our wildlife criminology discourse – one that encompasses a range of wrongdoing and harm against non-human animals. Earlier in this chapter, we set out our definition of wildlife and for the purposes of developing wildlife criminology our definition of wildlife crime is similarly expansive. In addition to wildlife trafficking of live species and illegal killing of wildlife for 'sport', our conception of wildlife crime includes non-human animal baiting, illegal hunting, egg collecting, illegal predator control, taxidermy offences and illegal exploitation of non-human animals for food, medicine, ornaments and clothing. Nurse (2015: 27) offered the following definition:

> For an act to be considered to be a wildlife crime, it must:
> - be something that is proscribed by legislation;
> - be an act committed against or involving wildlife (as defined earlier) – wild birds, animals, reptiles, fish, mammals, plants or trees which form part of a country's natural environment or which are visitors in a wild state;
> - involve an offender (individual, corporate or state) who commits the unlawful act or is otherwise in breach of obligations towards wildlife.

This definition, updated to incorporate our earlier definition of wildlife (to include fungi, plants and farmed non-human animals of a wild species) broadly applies to our discussion of wildlife crime throughout this book. As Nurse (2015: 27) identifies, 'for the purposes of discussing wildlife law enforcement, wildlife crimes should also consider regulatory offences; breaches of the law which may not attract a punitive criminal sanction, but which nevertheless attract some sanction or enforcement activity'. Our discussion of wildlife 'crime' thus includes a broad range of harmful acts that encompasses direct and indirect acts or omissions and indicate failure to comply with legal obligations or comply with legislation, irrespective of whether the legislation or its associated sanction is distinctly criminal in nature or the species is actually living wild. Thus, non-human animal welfare offences committed against normally wild (in other words, undomesticated) animals, such as elephants and tigers living in zoos, would fall within our definition of wildlife crime and such non-human animal abuse would, in our view, certainly merit discussion within the context of a wildlife criminology.

Our expanded inclusion of non-criminal offences and their inquiry does not stop there. In keeping with the critical vein of green criminology, wildlife criminology as a project also investigates and interrogates harm that is legal, but in causing suffering and injury is worthy of further examination. Therefore, whereas wildlife crime refers to violations of criminal, civil and administrative statutes, wildlife criminology unpacks the causes, consequences and responses to all harms and crimes to wildlife. We argue this is essential to contribute to the cessation of the destruction and extinction of wildlife through legal and illegal means.

Why a wildlife criminology?

Wildlife are facing threats from human activity on numerous fronts. The International Union for Conservation of Nature (IUCN) surveys the population status of tens of thousands of species across the planet and breaks down the threats to species into several categories. Their 2015 report found that tens of thousands of species might be threatened with extinction because of the pressure placed on them and their habitats by humans (IUCN, 2015). Some of these threats are largely indirect, such as habitat destruction (which can also lead to the killing of wildlife) stemming from residential and commercial development, transportation infrastructure, agriculture and pollution. But for other threats like hunting, trade and trafficking, which the IUCN (2015) refers to as 'biological resource use', wildlife are the direct victims of human actions. A wildlife criminology is long overdue to address this individual suffering of other beings, which we advocate is worthy of attention on its own. The current dire situation of wildlife overall, though, makes a wildlife criminology even more important.

A study by Allan et al (2019) found that 23% (1,237 species) of the terrestrial vertebrate species for which the IUCN has data are affected by threats across 90% of their distribution area. Furthermore, 84% of the Earth's terrestrial surface experiences human impacts (Allan et al, 2019). This means that terrestrial vertebrates (though we can likely extrapolate this to terrestrial invertebrates as well) are facing extensive pressure to survive. Allan et al (2019) found that Southeast Asia in particular is undergoing severe levels of harmful human actions to wildlife. Overexploitation and agriculture are the main causes of biodiversity decline (Maxwell et al, 2016), which, obviously, means harms to wildlife. WWF's (World Wildlife Fund) (2018) *Living Planet Report* has similar findings. Findings from their Living Planet Index indicate that the 'average abundance of 16,704 populations representing 4,005 species monitored across the globe declined by 60%' between 1970 and 2014 (WWF, 2018: 18). The same is true in the oceans. Only 4% of the world's oceans are undamaged by human activity with 41% being seriously damaged (Consortium for Ocean Leadership, 2019). It is estimated that over 90 million tonnes of fish are taken from the oceans each year and this is unsustainable (Consortium for Ocean Leadership, 2019). Even after the adoption of fishing quotas – of CITES in 1975 and the Convention on Biological Diversity in the early 1990s – biodiversity continues to steadily decline (WWF, 2018). In fact, the rate of human-induced species extinction is 100 to 1,000 times higher than non-human caused extinctions (Wilson, 2016), and while the main cause of species extinction is habitat loss, the second cause is overexploitation, poaching and the international illegal wildlife trade (CITES, 2016; IUCN, 2016; WWF, 2017). Human consumption of wildlife, then, is responsible for both biodiversity decline and extinction, whether that consumption is legal or illegal.

Climate change adds another dimension to an already bleak picture. Changes to terrestrial and aquatic habitats and ecosystems stemming from the ecological changes brought about by climate change means that wildlife face the additional threat of an unstable, unpredictable biosphere (WWF, 2018). Clearly, the sciences – climatology, physics, ecology and so forth – are working to develop mitigation and adaptation strategies to climate change and other environmental threats. This cannot, however, occur in isolation from the social sciences, where the expertise about what drives human behaviour and the ways in which harmful (and criminal) behaviour can be changed are critical to tackling climate change and threats to wildlife. It is one of the main reasons why there is a need for a wildlife (and climate change) criminology, which can contribute to preventing and reducing wildlife victimisation. As mentioned, the explorations of wildlife criminology are largely underpinned by four themes – commodification and exploitation, violence, rights, and speciesism and 'othering' – that cut across the topics of all the chapters.

Key themes of wildlife criminology

Commodification and exploitation

A common theme integral to harm against wildlife is their commodification. As detailed in Chapter 2, wildlife are considered to be human property. The status of non-human animals as human property and as exploitable natural resources plays a significant role in the extent to which wildlife are protected and harms visited on wildlife are classed as 'crimes'. Laws protecting non-human animals tend to give priority or enhanced protection to companion animals, meaning those animals who share homes with humans, over the protection of wildlife.

This often remains the case even in those areas where wildlife are subject to conservation efforts, such that wildlife are afforded legal protection that either limits the uses to which wildlife can be exploited or prohibits certain methods of killing or taking wildlife. As mentioned, wildlife protection legislation usually creates offences in respect of the illegal taking, killing and/or subsequent use of wildlife, but can be silent on the topic of wild non-human animal welfare. Wildlife's status is equivalent to a piece of furniture or other inanimate object that can be bought, sold and owned. Being regarded and treated as property enables much of the exploitation of wildlife. Wildlife are kept in aquariums, zoos and circuses (Chapter 2) and used in blood sports (Chapter 4).

Chapter 4 conducts an examination of shooting, fisheries, game and poaching, identifying that legal exploitation goes hand in hand with illegal acts. This chapter also examines non-human animal 'sports', such as bull-fighting, which largely depend on violence towards non-human animals and the spectacle of seeing an ostensibly 'wild' animal 'competing' in activities alongside humans. While the use of non-human animals for 'entertainment' and educational purposes is legal when carried out in accordance with regulations, there is considerable evidence of ongoing abuse of non-human animals in these areas (Van Tuyl, 2008; Linzey, 2009; Nurse, 2013). This includes the commission of non-human animal welfare and cruelty crimes that would fall within discussions of crime and deviance that should be considered by mainstream criminology, but which are frequently relegated to discussion within environmental, animal or human-animal studies discourses. Ownership and control are powerful concepts explored through Chapter 2's examination of how humans determine both the value of wildlife and the extent to which notions of harm, whether intentional or unintentional, are endemic to non-human animal use, as well as in Chapter 3's exploration of food and Chapter 4's investigation of sport.

As alluded to, commodification and exploitation go beyond entertainment and sport. As discussed in Chapter 3, wildlife are also a source of food and medicine. Whether it be subsistence hunting of game and bushmeat or luxury dining on caviar and songbirds, wildlife as part of the human diet is a complicated mix of survival, tradition, status-seeking and speciesism. The exploitation evidenced in wildlife as food stems from two aspects. First, there is the excessive consumption of individual wildlife, where their populations cannot survive so much loss. Thus, some wildlife species being consumed for food are facing extinction despite, in many instances, regulations designed to curb the overexploitation of wildlife for human consumption. Second, hunting and capturing practices are often cruel (though frequently legal), causing unnecessary suffering in order to increase the enjoyment for the people eating the wildlife. Commodification and exploitation violate species justice on both the individual level of causing non-human animal suffering and at the systemic level of entire structures or industries in society revolving around the harmful, unsustainable consumption of wildlife. Such harm is a form of violence that permeates discussions in wildlife criminology. The theme of violence in wildlife criminology also appears in other contexts of the human–wildlife interaction.

Violence

In addition to violence being inherent when wildlife are commodified and exploited as property, food and entertainment, violence perpetrated by wildlife and/or violence against wildlife also feature within humans' perceptions of themselves and within inter-human actions. Chapter 5 examines the notion that human violence has its origins in the violence evident in our evolutionary history. The prevailing wisdom is that wildlife are themselves violent, and when humans act violently they are behaving 'like animals', with the use of this value-laden language indicating notions of savagery and inhumane behaviour (Dubois et al, 2017). The exploration in Chapter 5 covers examples of violence by wildlife, including war among chimpanzees and rape by elephants. In contrast, the chapter also provides examples of altruism in wildlife, which counters the notion of human compassion as one of the exceptional characteristics setting us apart from the rest of the animal kingdom. The chapter aims to further challenge anthropocentric legislation by exemplifying common characteristics between wildlife and humans, and in so doing set the scene for a further chapter's exploration of wildlife rights.

Chapter 6 explores the links between non-human animal abuse and inter-human violence, with a specific focus on the extent to which harm caused to wildlife may be an indicator of violent tendencies and a predictor of future violence between humans (Linzey, 2009; Gullone, 2012). The links between non-human animal abuse and human violence have largely been explored within the context of companion animals (Linzey, 2009; Plant et al, 2016). Experts estimate that from 48% to 71% of battered women have pets who also have been abused or killed, and the link between domestic animal abuse and human violence is widely recognised by scholars and law enforcement professionals. At its most basic level, the link is discussed within the context of the progression thesis (MacDonald, 1963; Beirne, 2007), which essentially argues that non-human animal abuse is practice for later human violence. This chapter focuses on one aspect of the link: that concerning wild non-human animals and the extent to which wild non-human animal abuse can indicate a propensity or inclination towards other forms of violence. The species justice approach of green criminology (Benton, 1998) proposes that freedom from such violence needs to be considered when exploring the rights, or lack thereof, of wildlife.

Rights

As Chapter 7 of this book explores, the status of non-human animals as human property plays a significant role in the extent to which wildlife is protected and in how crimes (and harms) against wildlife are defined (Wise, 2000; Nurse, 2013). The notion of wildlife as something for human exploitation rather than someone (sentient beings) who should be protected for their own intrinsic value informs the nature of much wildlife protection and the regulation of human–wildlife interactions. Generally speaking, wildlife are considered to be a resource and available for human use, subject to regulation. In this respect, human concerns take priority over wildlife rights and the harms inflicted on wildlife are arguably minimised and marginalised.

Within our wildlife criminology discourse, we examine the notion of wildlife rights as something to be considered as slightly separate from the notion of non-human animal rights. Within a 'pure' conception of non-human animal rights, an argument might be made for non-human animals to be provided with rights broadly commensurate with those afforded to humans. In making a case for non-human animal rights, Singer ([1975] 1990) distinguished between legal rights comparable to human rights and the notion that humans and non-human animals have equal interest in avoiding suffering and so humans should apply equal consideration to non-human animals, making moral choices that try to avoid non-human animal suffering wherever possible. In Singer's conception, non-human animals of different species arguably have different interests and so there should also be different levels of protection for different non-human animals. As this chapter identifies, this conception already exists in the distinction between the protection afforded to companion animals through non-human animal welfare and anti-cruelty statutes that affect non-human animals under human control (companion and farmed animals) compared with the protection afforded to wild non-human animals. Some companion animals have their individuality recognised through measures such as the UK's Animal Welfare Act 2006, which recognises individual behaviours and needs in a manner that provides a form of non-human animal rights (Nurse and Ryland, 2014; Nurse, 2016b). However, wild non-human animals are arguably subject to a different regime, one that directly allows their continued commodification and exploitation and arguably seeks only to regulate the most excessive and violent of human activities that harm wildlife.

While this book is not directly engaged in non-human animal rights discourse, it actively considers in its exploration of commodification and exploitation, violence, and speciesism the impact of harmful human activities on a notion of rights for wildlife. Much of human–wildlife interaction centres on supposed 'wildlife management'. Gamborg et al (2012) suggest that there are two core approaches to wildlife management: the wise use of nature and the preservation of nature. Both approaches reject the unthinking marginalisation or destruction of wildlife. However, Gamborg and colleagues (2012) suggest that '[t]he wise use approach aims to accommodate humanity's continuous use of wild nature as a resource for food, timber, and other raw materials, as well as for recreation.' The idea of wise use appeals to our own best interests or to the interests of humans over time, including future people (this approach is often called 'sustainable use'). The goal of management is to enhance and maintain nature's yield as a valuable resource for human beings. For the preservationist, however, pristine protection of nature is the goal with the idea of allowing wild places to exist on their own. The former (wise use) conception arguably reflects the dominant ideological approach to wildlife use, whereas the latter (preservationist) approach arguably reflects a conception that more readily encompasses wildlife rights. A notion that wildlife and wild places should be largely left to their own devices also incorporates the idea that wildlife should be allowed freedom within their own territories and should broadly be free from human interference (Monbiot, 2013). While we acknowledge that the wise-use perspective will likely continue to dominate conservation management processes, we adopt a critical discourse approach to consideration of how such use negates any notion of wildlife rights. In doing so, we explore the notion that legal wise use and illegal activity frequently exist in a symbiotic relationship. An important part of the overall debate about wildlife and non-human animal rights is which wildlife have the right to rights? Even the most vocal advocates, such as Steven Wise and his Non-Human Rights Project, focus on mammals, particularly those considered to be sentient, while largely remaining silent with regard to other species.

Speciesism and 'othering'

As mentioned, underpinning much legislation is the anthropocentric notion of wildlife as a resource that can legitimately be exploited by humans, subject to considerations of sustainable use and minimising the cruelty involved in wildlife exploitation. Thus, debates around wildlife protection are socially constructed and reflect the idea that wildlife protection and classifications of non-human animals in legal terms is carried out according to human concerns. As White and Heckenberg (2014: 121) explain, 'animals are valued by humans in a highly stratified way. Put simply, we like some, we hate some, and some we don't really care or think about.' Clearly, this is reflected in legal protection, which provides different levels of protection to different non-human animals according to anthropocentric calculations of 'value'. White and Heckenberg further explain this point, identifying that we socially construct notions of those wildlife. Not only are some species deserving of our protection while others are not, but also some species are considered to be attractive and thus 'deserving' of protection efforts, while other species, who may well also be endangered, rate lower within not only the public consciousness, but also that of the environmental non-governmental organisations, which drive much campaigning activity. Thus, 'saving the tiger is publicly popular, for example, stopping the killing of sharks less so' (White and Heckenberg, 2014: 123). Wyatt (2013a), when detailing wildlife trafficking, refers to this as the hierarchy of victimhood. Charismatic megafauna are the species most worthy of human attention and protection, whereas reptiles, fish and insects garner little, if any, acknowledgement. Plants are even further down the hierarchy.

This logic is extended further when considering wildlife that is classed as a 'pest' species. In these cases, such wildlife can be legally killed where it is considered to present a threat to human or non-human animal health, crops or livestock. The precise definition of wildlife as a pest is socially constructed and varies, dependent on jurisdiction, but generally operates according to broad definitions of species considered to be harmful to human health or interests (Hadidian, 2012; Beirne, 2014). Speciesism, then, is at the core of who is commodified and exploited, who the victims of human violence are, and who the subjects of rights are. Thus, speciesism and the 'othering' of wildlife occurs on two levels. First, humans place themselves as the focal point – humans are the most important species and everything else is lesser. Second, humans assign values to the 'others', considering some to be worthy of some protection from commodification, exploitation and violence and deserving of rights, whereas other species are not given these same considerations. Like Beirne's (2018) non-speciesist criminology, wildlife criminology seeks to highlight speciesism and challenge the harms and suffering that it perpetuates.

Towards a wildlife criminology

A more prominent acceptance within criminology is emerging, that wildlife crime represents a substantial contemporary problem. Various criminologists, both green and mainstream, recognise wildlife crime as one of the major global crime problems existing today (Schneider, 2012; Wyatt, 2013a; Nurse, 2015; Sollund, 2019). Benton (1998: 149) identified in one of the first dedicated special edition journals of green criminology that '[i]t is now widely recognized that members of other animal species and the rest of non-human nature urgently need to be protected from destructive human activities.' Thus, justice systems, enforcement practices, policy and criminological analysis need to consider more than just harms and crimes committed against humans, they also need to consider harms visited on non-human animals and the environment itself. However, 'criminology, as traditionally defined, is about human harms that are defined in criminal law, all other forms of harm tend to be excluded from criminology unless unorthodox approaches such as those found within critical radical criminology serve as the foundation for criminological analysis' (Lynch and Stretesky, 2014: 4). Thus, criminology still, largely, routinely ignores harms against non-human animals and environmental harms and gives scant attention to wildlife issues except in respect of some consideration of wildlife trafficking as an area of global crime (see for example Wyatt, 2013a; Nurse, 2015; van Uhm, 2016; Sollund, 2019).

This book explores wildlife within a broader criminological context, considering our relations with wildlife and the values, morality and rules that underlie human relationships with wildlife, as well as the regulatory structures and enforcement perspectives that deal with human offending against non-human animals. The various chapters in the book make the case for a wildlife criminology that identifies various harms against wildlife as a concern of both green criminology and something that mainstream criminology should consider. Harms against wildlife link to mainstream criminological concerns of deviance, violence and subversion of societal rules. Wildlife criminology also raises issues concerning policing, in both the narrow sense of how police agencies deal with wrongdoing and a wider sense of how society regulates issues that threaten social control. Our conception of wildlife criminology argues that examining harms and crimes against wildlife is integral to considering such notions.

In Chapters 2 through 7, we explore the four core themes of commodification and exploitation, violence, rights, and speciesism and 'othering' in relation to some of the current harms and crimes against wildlife. Chapter 8 explores likely forthcoming events and legal developments that could affect wildlife and wildlife protection. In particular, this chapter considers European Union law and the protection of wildlife in a post-Brexit world. The chapter also provides a roundup of developments in, for example, possible further bans on the fur trade and the debate on the 'militarisation' of wildlife conservation. Such a discussion of what the future threats to wildlife may be brings the discussion around to what the future of wildlife criminology may be and what as a complementary endeavour to green criminology, future wildlife criminological writings may contribute.

As already evident, throughout this book, we employ green criminological perspectives of ecological justice and species justice. Therefore, we consider both crime and harm as part of the wildlife criminology project and in doing so argue that wildlife criminology can be situated not just within green criminology but also within social harm discourse (Lasslett, 2010; Pemberton, 2016). That means future wildlife criminological research will undoubtedly expose harms and crimes against wildlife that have previously been ignored or invisible. Future writings and research may also solve the tangle of anthropocentric vocabulary and language, which we continue to use, though as mentioned, it perpetuates a human-centred, us-versus-them dialogue in many ways. Such future research also promises to propose new prevention strategies and disruption tactics to protect further the planet's severely threatened wildlife. Thus, the aim of a wildlife criminology is ultimately, even in the smallest way, to contribute to a healthier planet for wildlife and people, with less violence to our fellow creatures.

2

Wildlife as Property

This chapter examines the notion of wildlife as property or 'things' and critically analyses the extent to which anthropocentric notions of wildlife as a resource for human exploitation determines the harm caused to non-human animals. The reality is that wildlife, in common with other non-human animals, are often defined as 'things' akin to property, in a manner that allows for their continued exploitation for human purposes and for the minimisation of societal condemnation of harm suffered by non-human animals.

For wildlife criminology, this raises issues regarding the extent to which both harms and crimes against non-human animals might be considered 'victimless' crimes and fall outside mainstream criminological inquiry. The status of wildlife as property influences the extent to which wildlife is protected by legal systems as well as the consideration of wildlife crimes as deserving of criminological or law enforcement attention. Wildlife, living outside human control, are arguably protected less than companion non-human animals whose legal protection reflects their close proximity to humans and habitation under human control (Schaffner, 2011; Nurse and Ryland, 2013), and are protected only so far as their interests coincide with human interests. Arguably, notions of crime are socially constructed such that what is defined as crime varies across jurisdictions and societies (Nurse, 2013; White and Heckenberg, 2014). In respect of harms against wildlife, a range of factors determines the seriousness afforded to such harms, including cultural and religious beliefs, legal classifications, type of non-human animal involved and type of harm. However, anthropocentric concerns frequently underpin the extent to which wildlife crimes are taken seriously within a particular jurisdiction. In respect of enforcement activity, the narrow distinction between legal and illegal activity, the nature of wildlife protection legislation and even ideological issues concerning the efficacy of enforcement can be factors in determining how and by whom wildlife harms are investigated and prosecuted (Nurse, 2011, 2013).

These issues are of importance to the wildlife criminology project, as many of the crimes committed against non-human animals who are 'owned' or are kidnapped to become 'owned' are linked to activity that is ostensibly legal. Nurse (2013: 1) used the term 'animal harm' to cover a range of activities directed at non-human animals, but which inevitably result in some form of harm whether physical or psychological. As outlined in our definition of wildlife criminology (see Chapter 1), this chapter is concerned with the harms caused to non-human animals within what are primarily legal activities, identifying that the failures of regulated industries that use non-human animals often have serious consequences for non-human animals. Such consequences and the harms that inflict them are of interest to our conception of a wildlife criminology; an exploration of crime, deviance or neglect of non-human animals that results in unlawful activity and subsequent harm to wildlife.

This chapter examines how anthropocentric notions of morality and human-centred values underpin the exploitation of non-human animals and the sense in which they are 'owned'. Employing a green criminological perspective, the chapter examines the use and abuse of wildlife within the non-human animal 'entertainment' industry, such as aquariums, zoos and circuses, and examines both the legality of this use and the 'animal harm' contained within such uses (Nurse, 2013). Evidence exists, for example, of psychological harm caused to wild animals in zoos that would likely be unlawful if experienced by companion non-human animals. Yet, zoos and safari parks are ostensibly legal operations representing officially sanctioned exploitation of wildlife. Thus, animal welfare legislation is often the only mechanism through which action can be taken in respect of what would otherwise be deemed unlawful captivity (see Chapter 7 on animal rights). We end the chapter by touching on how wildlife come to be property – that is, a short discussion of the wildlife trade, including the online market.

Non-human animals as property

While Chapter 7 discusses the concept of animal rights in more detail, the classification of non-human animals as 'things' and as human property is important to note in respect of our discussion of a wildlife criminology. Arguably the two concepts (rights and status) are inextricably linked as several non-human animal rights advocates argue that effective protection for non-human animals relies on human legal rights being extended to non-human animals (Wise, 2000; Beirne, 2007, 2018). Our later discussion (Chapter 7) explores this argument in respect of how providing rights for all sentient beings is arguably an effective way to address illegal activity. This is particularly the case in respect of cruelty offences where a positive assertion of rights (for example, the right to bodily liberty) as opposed to a negative 'protection from' harm approach can be deployed. This distinction can be more than cosmetic and provides scope for preventative legal activism to prevent action that could infringe on non-human animal rights as opposed to action taken only *after* a harmful act (such as non-human animal abuse) has taken place.

However, in this chapter we examine how legal constructions of non-human animals as 'property' arguably create circumstances in which non-human animal interests are ignored or marginalised within law and anthropocentric practices that harm non-human animals are prioritised. Wise (2000) argues that in respect of wild non-human animals, the notion of being 'legal things' is problematic because it differentiates the legal protection given to even the most trivial of interests of human beings and that afforded to other sentient species such as bonobos, chimpanzees, gorillas and orang-utans. In a legal sense 'their most basic and fundamental interests – their pains, their lives, their freedoms – are intentionally ignored, often maliciously trampled, and routinely abused' (Wise, 2000: 4). Essentially, there is no need to grant rights to 'something' that is 'owned' as the core consideration for legal systems would be the 'property rights' of the owner. Nurse and Ryland (2013: 10) argued that 'theories relating to animals as property argue that animal welfare benefits those who have an investment in animals as property (including farmers, livestock producers and retailers), because healthier animals maximise return on their investment'. Rollin (2006: 155–6) identifies that non-human animal protection and anti-cruelty laws 'take the people who own or use animals as primary objects of moral concern, rather than the animals themselves'.

Thus, legal systems are concerned with protecting the 'property rights' of owners and where a non-human animal is injured or harmed, recourse is often provided to the owner for the harm or loss they are perceived to have suffered rather than the harm caused to the non-human animal. For wildlife criminology, our concern is that the focus of the harm (that is, injury to a non-human animal) is being ignored and under-appreciated within our overall conceptions of crime and harm and specifically within criminal justice systems. More worryingly, our understanding of harm, crime and the extent of societal violence is based on a value-laden system that risks classifying some forms of harm and serious abuse as minor or tolerable, based on discriminatory (speciesist) notions of what constitutes a 'worthy' victim.

This book's notion of wildlife criminology is concerned with how the status of non-human animals as 'property' also influences law enforcement discourse in respect of wildlife and wildlife crime. Moore (2005: 91) argued that '[non-human] animals who have been abused do not have their interests represented in court. Instead, the state alone is able to prosecute crimes against [non-human] animals.' Moore's contention is, in part, that the failure of (US) courts to recognise non-human animals as crime victims means that their victimhood status and needs are not adequately considered in criminal proceedings where the criminal harm (for example, abuse) is visited directly on the non-human animal. In this respect, non-human animals' status is different from that of other crime victims who are frequently able to advocate on their own behalf via such mechanisms as victim impact statements or direct engagement with investigators or prosecutors concerning the harm they have suffered.

However, a more fundamental legal issue exists as within most jurisdictions, non-human animals *cannot* be crime victims (Wellsmith, 2011). Thus, investigations, prosecutions and court processes do not directly engage with the suffering or harm caused to all sentient beings, but instead differentiate between human and non-human animals in a speciesist manner (Beirne, 2007; Sollund, 2019). This is problematic not just in the context of a flawed justice system that does not adequately consider all crime victims, but also because the harm being visited on a non-human animal may be part of an overall offending profile or pattern of behaviour. In short, our justice systems may be selective in terms of which crimes or harms committed by an offender are considered, with the consequence that our punitive and rehabilitative sentencing practices do not address the reality of an offender's actions or pathology.

In addition, our justice systems operate with a restricted notion of victimhood that arguably distinguishes between 'worthy' human victims and others such as non-human animals. Animals' status as the property of humans means that laws often require humane treatment and prevention of unnecessary suffering of non-human animals, but do not protect or take into account their interests (Francione 2007). This arguably reflects the reality that laws that create offences in respect of harms visited on wildlife also generally allow for their continued exploitation. Thus, while in one sense non-human animals are protected from certain harms and wildlife should be protected from unsustainable use that might lead to their extinction, the same laws still allow for certain levels of exploitation and recognise non-human animals as a resource under human control and provided for human exploitation and benefit. This means that non-human animal protection is not absolute; elsewhere, Francione (2007) identifies that economic, legal and social factors prohibit recognition of non-human animal interests unless a human interest (or benefit) also exists.

Wildlife criminology argues that we need to expand our definition of 'crime victim' and include wildlife within victimology discourse. Much of criminology is concerned with human victims and exclusively considers harms committed against humans. Understandably, criminology as a discipline is engaged in discussion of how to prevent or address crimes that have a negative impact on human lives. This is particularly the case in respect of crimes of violence that cause fear or distress and may even result in death. Such crimes are also the focus of much policing activity and Lea and Young (1993: 89) argued that 'the focus of official police statistics is street crime, burglary, inter-personal violence – the crimes of the lower working class'. However, those offenders involved with wildlife crime and wildlife harms may also be involved in other activities that fall within the remit of justice systems and that should bring their activity within the criminological gaze. However, wildlife as sentient beings and as the subject of human control will also be of importance to justice systems where activity that infringes regulations and legal protection takes place, irrespective of whether the harms are classed as crimes or other types of unlawful activity.

Legal status of wildlife

As indicated earlier, the legal status of wildlife as property is of importance to how crimes and harms against wildlife are dealt with by legal systems. A range of laws provides different types of legal protection for wildlife, containing general protections for non-human animals living in the wild, such as: prohibitions on certain methods of taking or killing wildlife; protection for non-human animals during breeding seasons; and protection for nests and other wildlife habitats. The precise laws in place may vary across jurisdictions, but are generally based on the notion that wildlife is a natural resource that can be taken and killed for human benefit including for subsistence (food or clothing) or for sport. However, legal exploitation of wild non-human animals is often inextricably linked to illegal exploitation and one challenge for wildlife management, control or sustainable use programmes is how to address illegal exploitation and non-compliance with legal controls or regulatory systems.

The legal status given to wildlife and how it is considered within different legal systems, clarifies which activities that harm non-human (wild-living) animals are classified as crimes. Radford (2001: 122) identifies that broadly (non-human) animal law has a number of aims, as follows:

- preventing cruelty and reducing suffering;
- improving non-human animal health (and as a consequence, human health);
- protection and conservation of wildlife;
- promoting non-human animal welfare and specifying what constitutes acceptable minimum welfare standards;
- securing public safety;
- safeguarding commercial interests encouraging responsible non-human animal ownership; and
- reflecting a moral consensus.

While Radford's analysis sets out the broad focus for (non-human) animal law, Nurse (2015: 20) identified that 'wildlife law is clearly concerned with species justice and the development of legal mechanisms to provide protection and punish harm and is also linked to environmental justice given that wildlife is, in some circumstances, a natural resource of some importance'. The underlying principle of wildlife legislation is that wildlife is primarily intended as natural resource or conservation legislation whose goal is effective management of wildlife as a resource. Thus, while wildlife law often specifies offences and punishments in relation to misuse of wildlife, it is often predicated on a presumption that continued exploitation of wildlife is allowed and expressly permitted within the confines of the law. Thus, laws may allow the killing or taking of wildlife for sport shooting purposes, while prohibiting the use of poisons or certain types of traps. In other words, the principle of killing wildlife is established by law, but controls over the cruel methods of killing or capture might be included in legislation where non-human animal welfare concerns may arise over certain methods (see also our discussion in Chapter 4). Potentially this is paradoxical and suggests inconsistency in concerns for wildlife. For our wildlife criminology project, we identify a need to rationalise wildlife law and to investigate the inadequacy inherent in its intended use as conservation or wildlife management legislation rather than as species protection and/or criminal justice legislation. National wildlife law, while implementing international and domestic perspectives on wildlife protection routinely allows the continued exploitation of wildlife (Nurse, 2012, 2015) and we contend that this possible paradox requires consideration of the harms that arise from inadequate wildlife protection regulation.

The conundrum of protection versus continued exploitation exists in the paradoxical status of wildlife as a natural resource that can be exploited while wildlife also serves as a natural resource that should be protected and held in trust for future generations. Historically, 'wild animals were seen as a *res nullius* public property' (Nurse, 2015: 65) or the property of 'no one' (Epstein, 1997). However, contemporary developments in law have meant that in most countries 'wild animals fell into the common class, meaning they belonged in common to all citizens (Schaffner, 2011: 19). Thus, wildlife can sometimes be referred to as being *res communis*. This distinction is an important one as the notion of *res nullius* suggests that 'such resources belong to no one and are therefore free for the taking' (Weston and Bollier, 2013: 127). However, contemporary sustainability perspectives contained in legal instruments like the 1982 World Charter for Nature and the 1992 Biodiversity Convention (the Rio Convention), require countries to protect wildlife for the benefit of future populations. This means that any use of wildlife should be on a sustainable basis, ensuring that populations of wildlife are not exploited to extinction. Nature conservation, environmental management and wildlife policies are required to embody these sustainability principles. Thus, 'national wildlife laws incorporate the notion of wildlife as something that should be preserved in trust for future generations' (Nurse, 2015: 65), and states will frequently constrain the rights of individuals to take wildlife to prevent overexploitation and possible extinction of wildlife populations.

In essence, wildlife becomes the property of the state or of private individuals who own the land and who are able to exert property rights over wildlife. The wildlife trust doctrine allows states to regulate hunting, fishing and other game activities in the interest of conserving state interests in wildlife as property of a state. For example, the US Supreme Court in *Hughes v Oklahoma* 441 US (1979) 'expressly confirmed that US states could implement in law their legitimate concerns over the need to conserve and protect wildlife within their borders' (Nurse, 2015: 66).[1] In principle, wildlife law incorporates green criminology's species justice perspective (Benton, 1998; Nurse, 2013; White and Heckenberg, 2014) of providing a legal means through which animal protection can be achieved and harms against animals addressed through legal systems. Where conflict exists between human and animal interests, wildlife law provides a means through which arguments that animals should be protected can be pursued before the courts.

Wildlife law is primarily a matter of public law; that is, the law which 'relates to the inter-relationship of the State and the general population, in which the State itself is a participant' (Slapper and Kelly, 2012: 7). Criminal law has become the default mechanism through which wildlife protection and punishment for violations is achieved in the majority of jurisdictions, not least because of the implementation requirements of the Convention on International Trade in Endangered Species of Wild Fauna and Flora (CITES) and classification of wildlife trafficking as a serious crime by bodies such as the International Criminal Police Organization (INTERPOL) and the United Nations Office on Drugs and Crime (UNODC). Situ and Emmons (2000) identify two types of criminal law: *substantive* and *procedural*. Substantive criminal law is typically contained within a state's criminal code which 'defines the "wrongful" behaviour of citizens and stipulates corresponding punishment' (Situ and Emmons, 2000: 19). In part, the goal of criminal law is social control; encouraging behavioural conformity by punishing behaviour considered to constitute a public wrong. In this context, criminal law is also socially constructed such that the precise content of criminal codes varies from jurisdiction to jurisdiction, reflecting each society's notion of acceptable behaviour, albeit some offences such as murder and theft against the person are universal crimes. Thus, the nature of criminal offences and punishments in respect of wildlife varies commensurate with each society's notion of wildlife's 'value', the need for its protection and a consensus on how wildlife offenders should be punished.

White (2008: 32) argues that what is determined as environmentally harmful is 'shaped by what gets publicly acknowledged to be an issue or problem warranting social attention'. Thus, the extent to which wildlife law forms part of or is subject to a jurisdiction's criminal code varies, as does the list of prohibited acts that are classed as crimes when committed against wildlife. White (2008: 37) identifies 'ambiguities of definition' to be a significant factor in defining environmental harm. Thus, while some policy makers might consider poaching to be a serious wildlife crime deserving of punishment through the criminal law, others might consider this to be a property crime, which can either be dealt with by the individual through the civil law or constitutes a 'lesser' regulatory offence worthy only of a fine. Integral to such judgements are policy attitudes towards wildlife offenders and recognition within the criminal justice and natural resources protection systems of wildlife criminality and the appropriate mechanism for dealing with wildlife crime (Nurse, 2015).

Schaffner (2011: 15) identifies that 'since the criminal law is designed to punish and deter immoral conduct, and the sanction is extreme, the intent of the individual violating the law is a primary element of the crime'. Wildlife law is replete with criminal law phrases such as 'intentionally', 'knowingly' or 'recklessly' when committing offences. This reflects the prevalence of assessing the deliberate nature of actions which affect wildlife within legal systems and the recognition of intent as a factor in wildlife criminality. Arguably, accidental actions that result in wildlife harm or death are excluded or minimised when considering offending although within wildlife criminology we would argue that the nature of the act and the resultant harm are of primary importance, not just intent and prior guilty knowledge. The wording of 'mainstream' criminal offences is also often used in relation with wildlife crimes. For example, von Essen et al (2014: 632) identify that illegal hunting which 'refers to the illegal taking of wildlife and wildlife resources' is sometimes 'stigmatized as theft'. Situ and Emmons (2000: 22) identify that 'the stigma of criminal conviction and punishment is one of the attractions of applying criminal law to environmental misconduct'. Criminal prosecution is a manifestation of the state on behalf of society and societal values, exercising power over citizens whose non-conformity with societal rules is deemed problematic. Offences against public laws, generally prosecuted by the state and inclusive of criminal offences that breach the duty owed to the general public, are subject to state sanction in respect of the 'social harm' or violation of the collective interest that the conduct of the breach exhibits, even though the harm may not be felt by all in society (Mann, 1992). Wildlife law, which reflects contemporary societal values that non-human animals are deserving of protection, usually contains sanctions which exhibit society's disapproval of non-human animal harm. However, sanction levels are variable with some wildlife offences attracting only fines, and fines at relatively low levels (Nurse, 2003). Where the option for prison sentences exists, these also tend to be at the lower end of the scale except where multiple offences have been committed or in respect of endangered or threatened species where penalties tend to be higher (Nurse, 2015).

Despite the perceived inadequacies in wildlife law sanctions (Wilson et al, 2007; Nurse, 2012) examination of wildlife law's basic enforcement framework and the intent of sanctions makes clear that wildlife law functions as criminal law in respect of those activities proscribed as offences in legislation. Thus, wildlife criminology would argue for such offences to be the subject of mainstream criminological attention as well as being included within our wildlife criminology discussion. Non-human animals who are the subject of wildlife crime represent victims unable to speak for or represent their own interests and requiring public or representative action to address victim needs (Hall, 2013). The state, with an interest in minimising harm to its natural resources, protects wildlife by enacting wildlife protection legislation and creating a punitive and deterrent mechanism for wildlife harm. Accordingly, the wildlife criminology project, while noting that wildlife technically holds the status of property, would argue for a review of wildlife protection laws and consistency in sentencing and punishment that reflects the nature of the harms caused to wildlife.

Animals in entertainment and exhibition

Wildlife is used in a variety of entertainment and public exhibition settings that raise criminological concerns about their exploitation and associated harm. In the 'entertainment' world, non-human animals feature in arenas such as circuses and in street performance where they are trained to perform a variety of activities for human amusement (Shani and Pizam, 2008; Schroepfer et al, 2011). In the exhibition world, animals feature in aquariums, zoos and circuses where their purpose is primarily to satisfy the anthropogenic gaze. Animals also take part in sporting activities such as horse racing and greyhound racing, although these activities are not a primary focus of our analysis given that animals are primarily bred in domesticated settings to satisfy such sports; thus, they fall outside the remit of our wildlife definition set out in Chapter 1.[2]

Entertainment and exhibition use of wildlife raises several concerns appropriate to our wildlife criminology project; both in the context of ethical concerns about the use or misuse of non-human animals and in respect of notions of harm and deviance that are associated with such non-human animal exploitation. Schaffner (2011) identifies ethical considerations in respect of using non-human animals for entertainment purposes. She identifies that on the one hand, domestic or companion non-human animals are arguably better suited to exhibition than wildlife due to their nature and temperament. Familiarity with humans and with the reality of confinement is also a significant factor.

On the other hand, Schaffner (2011: 96–7) identifies potential benefits for wildlife exhibition, namely that 'if the [non-human] animals are well cared for and the exhibition itself does not cause physical or emotional stress to the [non-human] animals, one could argue that the benefits outweigh the minimal harm to the [non-human] animals' thus exhibition can be justified. The crux of this issue is the notion of 'minimal harm' and the balancing of human and non-human animal concerns. Arguably, the harm inflicted on non-human animals within these industries (discussed later) raises concerns about the rights of wildlife in such settings. This is discussed in more detail in Chapter 7, albeit our focus in wildlife criminology is not to debate the ethics of animal use that is currently legal.[3] Schaffner (2011: 97) goes on to say, however, that once reduced to exhibition 'wild animals by definition are no longer wild but captive and this change in their environment itself causes substantial harm'. In addition, there is considerable evidence of harm in non-human animal husbandry practices, which we explore further as we discuss the use of non-human animals in specific settings.

Aquariums, circuses and zoos

Shani and Pizam (2008) identify that growing awareness of animal rights, changing public opinion and the influence of animal rights movements is forcing animal attractions to re-evaluate their attitudes toward the use of non-human animals. Historically, non-human animals in aquariums, circuses and zoos provided a rare opportunity for the public to view the 'exotic other', non-native wildlife who might otherwise have remained remote and unseen. However, in a globalised interconnected world, eco-tourism provides a means to both view and contribute to the conservation of wildlife (Fennel, 2008; Honey, 2008). In addition, the wide availability of free wildlife visual material in the form of documentary film and television series, and short natural history and wildlife tourism clips on television, in cinemas and online allows for consumption of animal images within a safe (and inexpensive) space. Exotic wildlife is thus within the reach of consumers without the need for reliance on institutions that exploit non-human animals for financial gain. However, aquariums, circuses and zoos remain in existence, notwithstanding concerns about animal harms committed within their walls.

The fascination with the exotic arguably helps aquariums and zoos to continue in an age where their continued exploitation of non-human animals should arguably give rise to public outcry. However, zoos arguably have reoriented themselves to also function as conservation centres, saving non-human animals from extinction in the wild by preserving them in captivity and, where possible, captive breeding them to ensure species survival (Tribe and Booth, 2003). Patrick et al (2007) identified that conservation and education feature prominently in the mission statements of North American zoos. The original World Zoo Conservation Strategy (IUDZG/CBSG, 1993) defined the core objectives for all zoos that wish to make a substantial contribution to conservation as:

- actively supporting conservation of endangered species through coordinated programs;
- offering support and facilities to increase scientific knowledge that benefits conservation; and,
- promoting an increase of public and political awareness of the need for conservation.

However, Conway (2010) identifies that while zoos and aquariums exhibit many rare species, few are sustained for long periods due to demanding genetic, demographic and behavioural requirements. In reality, zoos are limited by the extent to which they can truly conserve threatened species as 'the scope for species conservation through captive breeding is limited by the availability of space and resources; and problems of husbandry, reintroduction, cost, domestication, and disease' (Leader-Williams et al, 2007: 237). Thus, conservation arguably becomes 'preservation' with the majority of zoos putting their resources into maintaining the collections that they have and drawing attention to the plight of rare and threatened species within their collections. A small number of zoos and parks are actively involved in conservation efforts that result in the reintroduction of threatened species back into the wild. However, as the authors of this book have noted elsewhere in relation to wildlife crime (Nurse, 2013, 2015; Wyatt, 2013a), unless adequate protections and enforcement exist for wildlife, they will continue to suffer harms and threats to population levels primarily through human-caused predation and exploitation. In this case, reintroduction may be inadvisable and the preservation and education approach may be a necessary evil of the zoo industry. Wickins-Dražilová (2006) argues that the continuing existence of zoos and their 'good purposes', such as conservation, science, education and recreation, can be ethically justified only if zoos guarantee the welfare of their animals.

But unfortunately, zoos have a long history of alleged animal welfare abuse identified through undercover investigations by animal welfare non-governmental organisations (NGOs) (World Animal Protection 2016; Lowe et al, 2019). Such investigations have identified that wild non-human animals kept in captivity can be caused considerable stress from being kept in unsuitable surroundings and by cruel practices employed by zoos in their treatment of their non-human wards. Veasey et al (1996) identify that while captivity naturally alters non-human animal behaviour, when comparing wild and captive behaviour regarding animal welfare, there is a need to identify behaviours that are most important to the animal and to assess the extent to which 'behavioural needs' are being suppressed by captivity. Clubb and Mason (2003) note that some species, including Asian elephants and polar bears, are prone to problems that include poor health, repetitive stereotypic behaviour and breeding difficulties, and generally fail to adapt to life in captivity. In part, this reflects the reality that such species are used to roaming over vast territories in the wild and forced adaptation to captivity may be challenging. Assessing the harm caused to non-human animals via captivity in zoos is potentially problematic. Mellor (2016) suggests that welfare considerations may need to go beyond the 'five freedoms' given that non-human animals can experience a range of negative effects that include anxiety, fear, panic, frustration, anger, helplessness, loneliness, boredom and depression.[4] Mellor suggests that, for example, non-human animals can be affected by threatening, cramped, barren and/or isolated conditions, which may give rise to welfare concerns in zoos.

Non-human animal circus performers have particular welfare concerns given that they are often kept in close confinement when not performing and are also subject to the rigours of travel between different performance sites. The suitability of non-human animals such as elephants, lions and tigers for circus life and performance is also questionable, given that non-human circus animals perform a repetitive range of stereotypical behaviours within their performance routines and thus are arguably denied the ability to perform natural behaviours. Thus, arguably, circuses are inherently problematic in terms of the commodification of animals and a notion of 'othering' that views them not for their intrinsic value, but as a performance product. Iossa et al (2009: 129) also identified that 'inadequate diet and housing conditions, and the effects of repeated performances, can lead to significant health problems. Circus animals travel frequently and the associated forced movement, human handling, noise, trailer movement and confinement are important stressors'. Evidence suggests that non-human circus animals are routinely kept shackled when not performing or caged for travelling, yet arguably open paddocks or other enclosures that provide for movement, play and the ability to exhibit at least some normal behaviours would be more appropriate (Schmid, 1995) and consistent with the principles of the five freedoms. However, the reality is that circuses may lack the space and resources to effectively provide for non-human animal welfare and so welfare concerns remain an issue. Given such welfare concerns and campaigns against circus exploitation of non-human animals, several countries have introduced bans on animals in circuses (Rook, 2011), although many have yet to do so and instead implement legislative measures intended to provide for the good treatment of wild animals in circuses. In the UK, for example, The Welfare of Wild Animals in Travelling Circuses (England) Regulations 2012 provides that circuses that use wild animals should be licensed. Condition 7 of the licence 'requires the operator to take all reasonable steps to meet the needs of wild animals in the travelling circus and to reflect good practice' (Defra, 2012: 4). Guidance supplied by the UK government's Department of Environment Food & Rural Affairs (Defra) indicates a need to maintain good standards of animal welfare. This is described as follows:

> It is important that the circus has sufficient veterinary cover to ensure that health and welfare needs of licensed animals are being appropriately met. This will involve travelling circuses working with their vets to ensure that all appropriate care is given to the animals, that all records are kept up to date and that veterinary advice and treatment is acted upon and recorded.
>
> The licensee must arrange as many visits, to be undertaken by a suitable veterinary surgeon, as are necessary to ensure the health and welfare of the animals.
>
> The licence holder must provide prompt treatment for sick or injured animals (irrespective of other visits and inspections that have been arranged). (Defra, 2012: 14)

In theory, these conditions provide for appropriate standards of animal welfare that would minimise harm. However, the standards employed are not those of an objective, enforceable standard of animal welfare. Instead, operators are required to employ 'all reasonable steps' and to accord with 'good practice', which arguably means good practice within the industry. The British Veterinary Association (BVA), together with the Born Free Foundation, the Captive Animals Protection Society and the RSPCA produced a briefing note labelling the regulations as 'ineffective and unenforceable' (BVA, 2012). The briefing argued that the welfare needs of non-domesticated, wild animals cannot be met within a travelling circus.

From our criminological perspective, there is considerable evidence of animals in circuses being subjected to treatment that contravenes the law and thus constitutes unlawful harm. NGOs have long held that training methods for circus animals are both morally cruel and also frequently contravene animal welfare legislation (Carmeli, 1997, 2002; Tait, 2011). Some evidence to corroborate these claims is found in the form of undercover footage taken by NGOs and in the detail of prosecutions for animal cruelty or failure to comply with regulations. For example, in the legal case of *William Joseph Vergis* 55 Agric. Dec. 148 (1996) the respondent engaged in business as a circus exhibitor, without a licence, and failed to handle a dangerous animal (a Bengal tiger) so that there was minimal risk of harm to the animal and to the public. Further evidence is routinely provided in media coverage of scandals involving poor treatment of non-human animal circus performers (see for example, Carter, 1999; Wilkes, 2012; PETA, 2019). As property, wildlife can be held captive and then used as exhibits or performers to satisfy anthropocentric notions of entertainment and as acceptable use or exploitation of wildlife. Until this fundamental relationship with other species changes, such establishments are likely to continue in some form.

Becoming property: wildlife as an industry

Certainly, a portion of the wildlife in zoos, aquariums, circuses and so forth have been born in captivity. There are live wildlife, though, that have been taken or kidnapped from the wild. The acquiring of live wildlife is one of many aspects of the wildlife industry. The wildlife industry includes entertainment venues as well as food, medicines, processed commodities and collectors' items (Wyatt, 2013a). The legal and illegal wildlife trade meets the demand for wildlife in these various aspects of the industry. The illegal wildlife trade – or wildlife trafficking – is a multi-stage process that begins in source countries, where wildlife are kidnapped or murdered to be smuggled either while alive or dead as a product (for more detail see Wyatt, 2013a; van Uhm, 2016). The legal wildlife trade runs in parallel; the only difference is one of legality – the human exploiting the wildlife has permission to do so when acting legally. The scale of wildlife trade is enormous with hundreds of millions of endangered species being legally traded each year through the permit system of CITES (no date). This does not include the other hundreds of millions of wildlife being traded that are not protected by CITES. Integral to legal and illegal wildlife trade is that once the wildlife is acquired it becomes the property of the person who has possession of the wildlife.

Of course, in our digital age, the internet plays a major role in meeting the demand for legal and illegal wildlife. Wildlife and wildlife products are sold through eBay, Facebook, WhatsApp, national social media outlets and so on. Whereas there have been efforts to ban sales of live wildlife (and non-human animals) from these digital platforms, the location, scale and scope of websites means that regulating or policing the sales of banned or illegal products – wildlife or otherwise – is a monumental task. In terms of illegal wildlife being sold online, Lavorgna (2014) identified that the internet facilitates trafficking in five ways by providing: mechanisms for communication and management of the illegal wildlife; information and technical opportunities for acquiring and selling illegal wildlife; organisational and relational opportunities between criminals and organised crime groups; promotional opportunities, such as fairs and other events in the physical world; and persuasive opportunities, which Lavorgna explains to be the chance to assure the potential buyer of the legitimacy or legality of the wildlife product. The internet further complicates the issue of non-human animal welfare, in terms of the ethics of selling live sentient beings online as well as the mechanisms of transport that are then utilised for people to receive their 'property'.

The legal and illegal wildlife trade, in general, further compound non-human animal welfare concerns. In the case of CITES-listed species, the Convention actually has very little to say regarding welfare. The main aspect covered is the transport of live wildlife. Importing countries should ensure the recipient of a living 'specimen' is suitably equipped to house and care for the wildlife. For exporting countries, any living specimen will be so prepared and shipped as to minimise the risk of injury, damage to health or cruel treatment. By and large, the language is taken from the International Air Transport Association (IATA) regulations on shipping live non-human animals. When CITES-listed wildlife are found to be traded illegally during transport, further welfare issues arise during confiscation. Of particular importance to a discussion of wildlife as property, is that wildlife – even when found to be illegal – remain the property of the person/offender in possession of the wildlife. For instance, Wyatt (2013b) found that at London's Heathrow Animal Reception Centre a pair of confiscated CITES-listed ring-tailed lemurs had been held in captivity there for more than two years. This was because they remained the property of the person, who was transporting them illegally without CITES documentation. As the court case was ongoing, his property could not be given away or taken from him. Thus, these two lemurs were housed in a small cage, in an unsuitable facility, where they mated and had babies. While the processes followed by the courts and the Centre are in line with the law that views non-human animals as property, clearly, in practice, there is visible harm.

Legal and illegal: regulating animal harm

Anthropocentric notions of animals as property are contained within legislation that regulates non-human animal use. While it is not the focus of this chapter to exhaustively cover the law concerning wildlife, our consideration does extend towards examining the manner in which regulations and legislation create offences. As we have outlined, anthropocentric notions of morality and human-centred values underpin the exploitation of non-human animals and the sense in which they are owned. The status of animals as 'property' extends to wildlife, which is generally considered to be a resource of the state and one that can (or 'should') be exploited as a source of revenue and a contributor to gross domestic product. Such considerations allow for non-human animal use for 'entertainment' purposes such as in aquariums, zoos and circuses, as well as for sport hunting use (discussed further in Chapter 4). However, our analysis identifies that legal and regulated uses of non-human animals within the exhibition and entertainment industries also facilitates illegal use and raises welfare concerns. Investigation of non-human animal use in the exhibition and entertainment industries by NGOs and others has consistently revealed animal welfare abuses, poor standards of non-human animal husbandry and regulatory failure. Evidence of psychological and physical harm being caused to wildlife who have entered the exhibition industry is commonplace. Much of this abuse is contrary to current legislation and regulation, yet such uses continue, and arguably regulatory inspection and enforcement mechanisms remain under-resourced and largely inadequate to deal with these issues.

We began this chapter by explaining that legally, non-human animals are property and are generally denied crime victim status within legal systems. Thus, animal welfare legislation and regulatory mechanisms are often the only mechanism through which action can be taken to address the harms visited on wildlife within areas where they are directly exploited for human benefit and entertainment. From a wildlife criminology perspective, such harms require active consideration, and as we detail in Chapter 7 welfare legislation is not enough.

Notes

[1] It should be noted that the issue in *Hughes v Oklahoma* concerned commercial trade in wildlife. The US Supreme Court, while confirming that states may promote the legitimate purpose of protecting and conserving wild non-human animal life within their borders, also ruled that states could only do so in ways consistent with the basic principle that the pertinent economic unit is the nation; and when a wild

animal becomes an article of commerce, its use cannot be limited to the citizens of one state to the exclusion of citizens of another state.

[2] Arguably, horse racing, which consists of the training of wildlife brought into captivity for the purpose of the sport, is at least tangentially covered by our wildlife definition.

[3] At time of writing in early 2019, the use of animals in aquariums, circuses and zoos is legal, subject to compliance with the relevant regulatory regimes. However, there are a number of campaigns in place that seek to change the law, particularly in Global North jurisdictions. See for example the RSPCA's campaign to end wild animals in circuses at www.rspca.org.uk/getinvolved/campaign/circuses and also the One Green Planet campaign online at www.onegreenplanet.org/animalsandnature/5-ways-you-can-help-end-the-use-of-animals-in-circuses/. In Chapter 8 – the future of wildlife criminology – we discuss this further.

[4] The five freedoms are: freedom from thirst, hunger and malnutrition; freedom from discomfort; freedom from pain and disease; freedom to express oneself; and freedom from stress and fear. These are considered to be the basic hallmarks of good animal welfare.

3

Wildlife as Food

Introduction

The wildlife that people consume for food covers the range of the diversity of species. Wildlife as food is a complicated issue as not only does it include luxury 'exotic' foods like caviar, whale and bear paws, but also includes common species such as deer, rabbits and snakes. Adding to the complexity is that some species, like caviar, were at one time common, but because of over-exploitation and unsustainable consumption have become a luxury (Bronzi and Rosenthal, 2014). Or, in the case of some bushmeat[1] species, the wildlife may be a staple for people in the wildlife's home range, but a luxury product when transported thousands of miles to a diaspora market far from where the wildlife was kidnapped. In addition, even though a non-human animal may be common, such as the pangolin once was, consumption can still be considered a luxury (Pantel and Anak, 2010). The pangolin has been and still is a special meal in wildlife restaurants in parts of Southeast and East Asia.

Clearly, many human communities have historically been and continue to be reliant on wildlife for food. That reliance may stem from necessity that the wildlife is one of the few, if not the only, protein source available to people living in the wildlife's habitat. In addition, the reliance may be underpinned by many years of tradition in which particular wildlife feature in cultural traditions of a community and may even have significance for ethnic identity. Whereas in the first case, alternative protein sources may reduce the consumption of wildlife as food, in the latter case, consumption may be difficult to change and reduce. The reason why there needs to be a focus on reduction is because as Ripple et al (2019: 3) found in their study: 'Our results suggest that we are in the process of eating the world's megafauna to extinction.' They found consumption for vertebrates other than megafauna (mammals, cartilaginous fish and ray-finned fish weighing more than 100kg, and birds, reptiles and amphibians weighing more than 40kg) are also threatened because of human demand for the wildlife as food.

In this chapter, we will explore various aspects of wildlife as food. In the first section, we expand on the evidence that wildlife as food is a topic worthy of further (green) criminological attention. We then go on to investigate specific examples where wildlife is consumed as food to explore the various motivations of consumption. This will be followed by a discussion of caviar, where there is evidence of organised crime orchestrating this complicated global black market. We end this chapter by discussing the speciesism that is inherent in our food choices.

Harms and crimes

As mentioned, killing wildlife for food is contributing to declining populations and extinction (Ripple et al, 2019). The International Union for the Conservation of Nature (IUCN) maintains the data for the Red List – a comprehensive list documenting the status of species, for which data have been collected. The status of each species is arrived at by combining data about population numbers, habitat, range, reproductive characteristics and so forth. Species may be categorised as 'data deficient' if this information has not been collected or is unavailable. The status categories are Extinct in the Wild, Extinct, Critically Endangered, Endangered, Vulnerable, Near Threatened, and Least Concern. Ripple et al (2019: 3) determined that out of the 39,493 vertebrate species in the IUCN Red List (not including those where there were no data, or those who were extinct in the wild or extinct), '21% are catalogued as threatened and 46% have decreasing populations'. The 292 species of megafauna, though, as defined earlier, are faring far worse. Fifty-nine per cent of megafauna are threatened and 70% have decreasing populations (Ripple et al, 2019). Harvesting for food is a significant factor in the decline of all vertebrates, but particularly for megafauna. 'Meat consumption was the most common motive for harvesting megafauna for all classes except reptiles where harvesting eggs was ranked on top' (Ripple et al, 2019: 3).

Other reasons for harvesting megafauna in addition to meat are also for human consumption: for medicinal use, as unintended bycatch in fisheries and trapping; for live trade; and for various other uses of body parts, such as the use of skins and fins (Ripple et al, 2019). Worryingly, 64% of the threatened megafauna are listed on one of appendices of the Convention on International Trade in Endangered Species of Wild Fauna and Flora (CITES) (Ripple et al, 2019). Such listing means that these species are already under threat from exploitative trade and should either not be traded at all or traded within strict quotas. Either CITES is not being properly implemented, complied with or enforced, in the case of these megafauna, or nations are not taking the proper measures to ensure domestic consumption and trade are controlled.

Even protected species, then, such as CITES species, are threatened by humans' demand for meat. The level of consumption, not just of megafauna as Ripple et al (2019) detail, but for other vertebrates as well is contributing to an overall decline of wildlife around the world (WWF, 2018). If that were not enough reason for criminologists to research and develop prevention and detection strategies, the ways in which wildlife are captured and killed is also a topic worthy of criminological discussion because of the harm and suffering these techniques induce. Hunting, trapping and fishing, in their various forms, are all likely to cause the wildlife pain and/or stress. Hunters may use weapons – guns, and bows and arrows – that hopefully kill the target wildlife quickly. Trappers may use nets, snares, pits and leg-traps. Nets and pits, in particular, are intended to keep the wildlife alive so that they can be killed freshly for consumption. The means of killing the wildlife from the net or the pit may or may not be humane. There is a contested international trapping standard that says that when killing a non-human animal, the method of killing should be such that it achieves 'irreversible unconsciousness' within five minutes. Anything over that is considered cruel. However, five minutes is quite a long time and seems counter to animal welfare principles, which generally argue for swift dispatch. Snares, depending on whether wildlife is caught by the neck or leg, may kill the wildlife or, like leg-traps, simply hold the wildlife until the trapper returns. Wildlife can remain in snares or traps for long periods. During this time, they may cause further injury to themselves in trying to get free. They may also suffer further distress and harm from exposure and lack of food and water.

Fishing poses similar injuries through catching fish in nets, piercing them with hooks, or cutting the fins off of sharks and throwing their bodies back into the water. Both trapping and fishing also have the added harm that there are instances where wildlife not intended to be caught are captured. The bycatch may drown in the air or be injured and thrown back into the water, in the case of fish, or for terrestrial wildlife, be injured by the trap or snare and be killed anyway without being eaten. All of these methods of capturing and killing wildlife contain some degree of harm. While we recognise that people will continue to be motivated to consume wildlife as food, we propose methods be used that are the most humane and least stressful to the wildlife. In the next section, we explore what the motivations are for consumption.

Motivations

The motivations behind the consumption of wildlife are at the heart of this complex market. We suggest these motivations can be categorised according to preference, necessity, status seeking and tradition. Some people consume wildlife because of beliefs that wildlife taken from the wild has better flavour and/or properties that are conveyed to the person eating the wildlife (Momii, 2002). For instance, a person eats a wild bear paw because they believe it will give them strength. So even if the particular wildlife is raised in captivity and available for consumption, people may still choose to eat wildlife caught in the wild because by eating a wild non-human animal they will take on some of the essence of that species. As mentioned, many people consume wildlife out of necessity. Wildlife may be the only source of meat for some people, for example being integral to the diets of indigenous peoples. And still others may consume wildlife as a means of displaying high status. Finally, different from preference for wildlife, some people may consume wildlife as part of cultural practices and long-standing traditions. We will provide examples for each of these to explore this complex consumption further.

Bushmeat as preference and necessity

Bushmeat could be used as an example of each of the consumption categories – preference, necessity, status seeking and tradition – but we are highlighting the motivations of preference and necessity. The unsustainable consumption of wild meat has been referred to as the wild meat crisis (Milner-Gulland et al, 2003; Lindsey et al, 2013) or as the bushmeat crisis across central Africa (Van Vliet and Mbazza, 2011). Legally, bushmeat is usually regulated. If a species of wildlife is allowed to be hunted for bushmeat, this is likely to be restricted to certain times of year, certain times of day and a limited number of each sex. Bushmeat may also be restricted to those people directly consuming the wildlife for subsistence and not be permitted for commercial purposes (Van Vliet and Mbazza, 2011). Such restrictions have been put in place in Central Africa, in particular, because overexploitation of bushmeat species is linked to their population declines. Despite the regulations, 'bushmeat sales remain significant (between 30–90% of the catch) clearly showing that the law is largely un-respected' (Van Vliet and Mbazza, 2011: 46). We can confidently surmise that this is not only happening in Central Africa, but across the globe as the demise of biodiversity is global.

If the law is being disregarded and bushmeat continues to be hunted despite restrictions, there must be strong motivations behind people's consumption. According to Van Vliet and Mbazza (2011: 49), 'The desire to eat bushmeat can be explained by the taste, habit, tradition, prestige, ritual and nostalgia'. In Central Africa bushmeat appears strongly linked to its natural and cultural value, whereas in other parts of Africa, like Nigeria and Western Africa, bushmeat consumption changes depending on availability and price (Van Vliet and Mbazza, 2011). Other studies concur, although other factors are also identified. Wild meat consumption is affected by taste preference (Schenck et al, 2006; Baia et al, 2010), price (Wilkie et al, 2005), availability of wild meat and substitutes (Van Vliet and Mbazza, 2011), wealth (Godoy et al, 2010), income (Wilkie and Godoy, 2001; Parry et al, 2014), and market access (Chaves et al, 2017). Bushmeat is in demand at local levels, but also in urban areas and internationally (Chaves et al, 2018). While local consumption likely links to necessity, though possibly also to preference, urban and international consumption seem clearly linked to preference as bushmeat would not be readily available in these locations and there are most likely alternative food choices as well. For instance, cane rat has been found in farmers' markets in London suburbs (Lynn, 2012), though clearly there are other meat choices.

Two examples seem to support local consumption of bushmeat being a necessity rather than preference. The first example comes from surveys conducted with miners and individuals supporting the mining camps in the Democratic Republic of Congo (Spira et al, 2019). During the course of a three-month study, the majority of individuals surveyed living in the mining camps expressed a preference for eating beef, chicken and fish. Due to necessity of the situation though, these individuals hunted chimpanzees and gorillas. The miners similarly said that they would not hunt if they received a secure income, if there were domesticated sources of meat available, and if the hunting laws banning bushmeat were strictly enforced (Spira et al, 2019). Interestingly, hunting was made possible or at least easier due to the armed groups in the Democratic Republic of Congo. Having guns enables people to hunt great apes as well as contributing to a breakdown in law-abiding behaviour in the communities near to the bushmeat (Spira et al, 2019).

The second example where people eat bushmeat out of necessity rather than preference also comes from Africa. Madagascar is the home to dozens of lemur species, which are found nowhere else on the planet. Many of the lemurs are living in areas where the human population are suffering from malnourishment (Borgerson et al, 2017). In fact, it is estimated that 94% of lemurs are becoming extinct in such areas. People have turned to poaching the lemurs as they have no other protein source. The chickens they were trying to raise are infected with disease, which led to the reliance on wild meat (Borgerson et al, 2017). Vaccination of poultry and improved husbandry are part of the solution to take pressure off the wildlife.

At times, then, bushmeat is eaten, even though it is prohibited or regulated, because people prefer it for the taste and/or for the sense of nostalgia. Other times, people eat bushmeat because of the lower price or the lack of alternative sources of protein. Either way, the very concept of bushmeat raises interesting questions about how some wildlife come to be acceptable food and others do not. Furthermore, the naming of wild meat as 'bushmeat' from some parts of the world, but not from others, also raises questions about the value judgements placed on food consumption, particularly from the Global North or Western discourses. This is particularly evident in our next section, which investigates the consumption of songbirds in Europe for status seeking and tradition, the other two proposed categories of motivation for eating wildlife.

Songbirds as status seeking and tradition

Another definition of bushmeat is any non-domesticated terrestrial mammals, birds, reptiles and amphibians harvested for food (Nasi et al, 2008). Why the practice of capturing and eating migrating songbirds in parts of Europe is not referred to as 'bushmeat' speaks to the power of language in labelling consumptive behaviours in particular ways. The songbird market is not so different from the bushmeat market or from exotic meats like pangolin served in restaurants (Clements-Housser, 2017). Eating songbirds is a long-standing practice in Cyprus where it is called 'ambelopoulia'. The same takes place in parts of Italy and France. Songbirds, such as black caps, song thrushes and chiffchaffs among others are targeted by the songbird poachers. Songbirds migrate each year from Africa across the Mediterranean to northern Europe in the spring and then back again, going south for the winter (Clements-Housser, 2017). In Cyprus, poachers set up 'mist nets' along the songbirds' migratory routes to harvest the birds. They are called mist nets because the fabric of the net is very fine, making it practically invisible. In Cyprus in particular, poachers have planted acacia trees, which attract the songbirds and then purposely set the mist nets among the acacias to catch the songbirds (Clements-Housser, 2017). In addition, the poachers also hide speakers in the acacia trees which transmit bird calls to lure the songbirds to the acacia trees and into the nets.

These hunting practices are illegal, but until recently have largely been unchallenged. (Clements-Housser, 2017). Songbirds, like the *Emberiza hortulana* – ortolan bunting, which we will return to in a moment – have been protected in the European Union since 1979. But several countries, like France, where the tradition of eating songbirds is centuries old, did not ban hunting and eating of the birds until 1999 (Alderman, 2014; Im, 2018). Songbird protection may seem unnecessary as many are, like the ortolan bunting, listed on the IUCN Red List as Least Concern, though their populations are decreasing (BirdLife International, 2017). There are several reasons, though, why the practice was and should be banned.

The first reason to ban songbird hunting and consumption is that the sheer volume of the catch is unsustainable (Clements-Housser, 2017). Tens of thousands, hundreds of thousands, and sometimes millions of songbirds are captured each year during their migration (BirdLife International, 2017). Over time, this is bound to threaten the viability of the populations. The second reason is that some of the species of birds caught in the nets are not the target of the poachers (Clements-Housser, 2017). Mist-netting is an indiscriminate means of trapping and those species who are not going to be eaten are discarded or killed. Thus, as with bycatch in fishing and indiscriminate traps for hunting, the death toll of individuals is several times higher because of the methods used to capture the wildlife. The final reason to ban the consumption of songbirds is the suffering the songbirds are subjected to in order to fulfil the demand. Once the poachers have caught the songbirds, the songbirds are kept in cages in total darkness for 21 days (Alderman, 2014). Sometimes the birds are kept in caves or blacked-out rooms, but other times they are blinded to achieve the required darkness. The darkness is 'required' because it induces the songbirds to gorge (Alderman, 2014). So, for the final three weeks of their lives, they will eat as much millet and as many grapes as they are given. At the end of the three weeks, the fat levels of the songbirds have increased by three times (Alderman, 2014). The darkness, either because of the location or because of the blinding of the birds, can readily be seen as a harm that causes unnecessary suffering. The injury does not end there. The songbirds are then 'thrown alive into a vat of Armagnac brandy (which both drowns and marinades them), then roasted' (Im, 2018). The songbirds are cooked and consumed whole, following centuries of tradition (Clements-Housser, 2017).

Clearly, the consumption of songbirds falls outside the realm of necessity. The evidence that songbird eating is motivated by status seeking and tradition comes from both popular culture and from recent discussions in France. In 2018, the US cable television channel ran an episode of its drama series 'Billions', where the incredibly rich characters eat the thumb-sized ortolan bunting in the traditional way (Im, 2018). People – their heads covered with napkins – stick the whole bird, feet first, bones, beak and all into their mouths (Im, 2018). Apparently, the napkin over the head is to savour the aromas, enjoy privacy or hide the indulgence from God (Alderman, 2014). In this episode of 'Billions', the American celebrity chef, Wylie Dufresne, plays himself. Other well-known chefs – for example, Anthony Bourdain – have publicly admitted to engaging in this illegal consumption (Im, 2018). The importance of the involvement of chefs, in fiction or otherwise, is the decadence and extravagance that accompanies such a meal, thus displaying the high status needed to obtain and consume the songbird. Reports from France are that secret dinner parties are held, where songbirds are served (Im, 2018). This is likely to be true as 'About 30,000 wild Ortolans are still being culled illegally in the South of France every summer, while the police look the other way' (Alderman, 2014). Historically, the songbirds were only served to royalty and the elites and this appears to be a tradition that is being maintained (Im, 2018). Two French chefs, Michel Guerard and Alain Ducasse, have been campaigning to have the birds allowed on French menus for one week of each year (Alderman, 2014). Their rationale is it is important to preserve French culinary culture and that making consumption legal will reduce the price on the black market, which is around €150 per bird (Alderman, 2014).

The motivations behind consumption are diverse and not one or other. It is possible that preference, necessity, status seeking and tradition intertwine to drive people's consumption of wildlife. Understanding this complex interplay, though, is crucial to designing prevention and disruption strategies to help declining wildlife populations recover. The claim by the French chefs mentioned earlier about having a legal industry for protected species as a means to reduce black markets brings us to an ongoing contentious aspect of wildlife as food (and wildlife consumption in general). The existence of legal markets for food from wildlife may well provide the means to launder illegally sourced wildlife into the legal sphere. Or severely limiting a market may lead to a parallel black market to meet the demand. Both may be true as we see in the case of caviar, another complicated wildlife food market, which is further complicated by the involvement of organised crime.

Caviar

As mentioned, caviar is a particularly interesting food as it has undergone a social transformation from abundant and affordable to scarce and expensive. Caviar is also an interesting commodity because it sits across numerous cultures that place different values on food and that have different political and socioeconomic contexts that affect crime levels. Whereas caviar may be associated with Russia, which we will discuss in a moment, it may be less well known that in the US in the 1800s, both Atlantic sturgeon and shortnose sturgeon were hunted for meat and caviar (Sweka et al, 2006). The hunting was so excessive that by the early 1900s the populations of both species of sturgeon had decreased dramatically and fishing began to be regulated (Sweka et al, 2006). Atlantic sturgeon populations began to rebound with commercial fishing, commencing again by 1980 (Sweka et al, 2006). The resurgence was short lived. By 1996, Atlantic sturgeon populations had once again fallen, leading to a moratorium on commercial and recreational fishing (Sweka et al, 2006). In the case of the shortnose sturgeon, fishing only lasted until 1967; it was then that this species of sturgeon was listed on the Endangered Species Preservation Act 1966 (American Museum of Natural History, 2010). North American sturgeon species, and their close relatives – the paddle fish, which inhabits the Mississippi and other rivers – continue to be protected, but caviar trafficking is a problem for the survival of all of these species (Musing et al, 2019).

In the US, sturgeon fishing was a commercial operation not just for the few. Similarly, in Russia the tsars placed a caviar tax on fishing of sturgeon, probably establishing the fish roe as a luxury product, while at the same time it was sold cheaply in markets and consumed by the poor (van Uhm and Siegel, 2016). Caviar's status, at least in Russia and Europe, as fully a luxury product did not take place until the late 1700s, when it was specifically marketed to the European upper classes (see van Uhm and Siegel, 2016, for a detailed history of Russian caviar). After the creation of the Soviet Union in 1917, the Soviets controlled 90% of the world's caviar market (van Uhm and Siegel, 2016). Since the Soviets held a monopoly over the caviar trade, they could control the value of the market. Yet, while the Soviets kept strict controls on the market in terms of value and in terms of tightly regulating the viability of sturgeon stocks (van Uhm and Siegel, 2016), there also emerged a lucrative black market, which has been considered to be an inevitability in the Soviet socialist economy, where the lines between legal and illegal were often blurred and corruption and abuse of power were common (Siegel, 2005). To ensure the survival of the sturgeon, the Soviets banned fishing in the Caspian Sea in 1962 (van Uhm and Siegel, 2016). So, while for decades there was tight control, for decades there was also a parallel and intertwined criminal market. With the collapse of the Soviet Union in 1991, the strict control of the caviar market also collapsed and the decades-old criminal element of the caviar market became even more prominent.

> In the 1990s the caviar trade became extremely profitable. Not just legitimate business people, but especially *brakonieri* (poachers) started to fish for sturgeon on a massive scale and enormous amounts of cheap caviar appeared on the Russian market. This resulted in a decrease in the price of caviar, which in turn led to an increase in demand – from outside the production countries. (van Uhm and Siegel, 2016: 74)

The scale of illegality was – and still is – at times so extreme that entire Caspian Sea coastal communities function around illegal sturgeon fishing and the production of caviar (van Uhm and Siegel, 2016).

Interestingly, caviar trade was not integrated into the regime of CITES until 1998. Since then, specific measures govern the international caviar trade in addition to the standard procedures required of trade in CITES-listed species. In the case of caviar, this means there is an exemption of up to 125g for personal consumption, which an individual may carry between countries without CITES documentation. This might well be a means to flout CITES restrictions, by having numerous couriers carrying the allowed amount. For amounts more than 125g, the shipment must be accompanied by both an import and an export permit. And specific to caviar, the container in which the caviar is packed must be a tamper-proof container, which clearly shows that it has not been opened, and be affixed with a non-reusable label. Large shipments of caviar are often repackaged into smaller jars and the repackaging is required to follow the same standards (tamper-proof containers with non-reusable labels) and repackaging firms must be registered with CITES. The additional measures have led to fraudulent and forged containers and labels (Musing et al, 2019).

Caviar from the Caspian Sea remains under a moratorium, which presumably affects the global market price for caviar. The value of caviar has increased disproportionately to thousands of Euros per kilo because the declining sturgeon populations are making the product rarer and because of the involvement of various criminal groups in the illegal trade, who control, at least to some degree, the price (van Uhm and Siegel, 2016). Currently, concerns in the caviar trade centre on the burgeoning aquaculture portion of the market. Those who have been involved with caviar over the last few decades have said that the current owners of the aquaculture operations were the main criminals orchestrating the illegal trade. As has been witnessed for the Russian and former Soviet economies in general, much of the privatisation that took place when the Soviet Union collapsed gave profitable businesses to organised criminals (van Uhm and Siegel, 2016). Aquaculture is a means of laundering illegally caught wildlife caviar as legally farmed caviar, but also used as a way to 'blackwash'. '"Wild caviar is wanted" because it is rare and therefore special. The idea has taken hold that wild caviar, which is supposed to be "pure and all-natural", is of a higher quality than caviar from cultured sturgeon' (van Uhm and Siegel, 2016: 81).

Since wild caviar is very rare and largely illegal, legal caviar from aquaculture is being sold as illegal caviar. This maintains the status of the luxury product and the impression that the market is still viable. This shows the enmeshment of legal and illegal markets and, at least in the case of caviar, how criminal groups can use legal enterprises to hide their activities. 'In 2014 the illegal market is well-organized; its participants arrange for sales channels, transport, and bribes to be paid along the way (to the traffic police and customs officers). Senior government officials, fishery inspectors, police services and other agencies all have a stake in the business' (van Uhm and Siegel, 2016: 74).

This well-structured and corrupt pipeline is headed towards Western Europe, the major outlet for the caviar market (Musing et al, 2019). This is an important aspect of the caviar trade as so much of the international discourse, particularly with regard to demand and consumption of wildlife, is focused on Asia as the major culprit. But as an exploration of caviar highlights, as does the discussion of songbird exploitation and abuse mentioned previously, wildlife consumption for food is a global occurrence. Every region of the world is playing a part in the demise of the wildlife living there, by eating them – or at least some them – to extinction.

Speciesism

In a majority of countries, wildlife are the property of the state, so permission is likely to be needed to hunt or fish. There are instances, though, particularly for indigenous groups and those who are reliant on wildlife for sustenance, where hunting and fishing are allowed without a licence. Some wildlife, of course, are protected and are therefore not allowed to be eaten or consumed. The point is, wildlife are regarded as natural resources that people are permitted to use as the state deems appropriate (Weston and Bollier, 2013). Or people will continue to use wildlife as a source of food regardless of the criminalisation and/or harm caused by consumption. Yet, not all wildlife are treated the same and this is certainly the case when it comes to whether or not a society eats them. The different ways in which different cultures regard the various species of wildlife seem to stem from socialisation processes over many generations. The result is a hierarchy of regard for species not unlike the hierarchy of victimhood for wildlife from Chapter 1.

The speciesist hierarchy evident in the food chain looks different from that seen in other instances of victimisation. For food, in certain parts of the world, some species are removed from the food chain all together. Dogs and cats, for instance, are not eaten in the West, though this is a practice in parts of Asia. We bring domestic non-human animals into the discussion here to illustrate the speciesism. Does domestication make dogs and cats that much different from wildlife? Clearly, for many in the West it does. In the case of bushmeat, which wildlife are caught for food depends on where the hunting takes place and the cultural/social traditions that underpin such consumption. In Central Africa, people may eat other primates; in Europe, they may eat tiny songbirds. It is impossible, probably, to trace back to the origins of when a species first entered into the diet of a community. To most people in the West, eating a primate such as a chimpanzee or a gorilla is unthinkable. The Western hierarchy of species places primates and cetaceans (also eaten in some cultures) above other species, though likely to be beneath or on a level with companion animals.

The line between food and not-food becomes even more blurred when considering domesticated livestock and poultry. Cows, sheep, pigs, chickens and turkeys are not so different from wildlife. Yet, in Western society these species are considered acceptable to eat and 'game' species – deer, bear, rabbit – are consumed infrequently, if at all. In the West, dogs live in our houses, pigs make up dinner, and deer run in a few remaining 'wild' spaces. Wild food, except perhaps for fish, is a very small part of the consumption. Such physical and cultural distancing from wild food in the West probably stems from value judgements placed on other cultures, where dog, whale and primate/monkey are eaten. In these instances, the judgement is a moral one of harming a sentient being. Other judgements can be made too, though, as in the case of eating insects throughout Latin America. Here though, the judgement is one of disgust rather than a regard for the wildlife.

Wildlife as food raises other moral dilemmas for people concerned about welfare and rights of wildlife. In order to take the pressure off of wildlife in the wild, initiatives have been taken to farm wildlife. Some people are concerned, though, that bears and tigers, for instance, should not be subjected to farming conditions. Again, this highlights humans' speciesism: how is farming a bear or a tiger different from farming a pig or a cow? Other concerns raised are that farming of wildlife does not in reality reduce the pressure on wild populations. This stems from the preferences, as outlined earlier, for wild-caught meat, which means a farmed alternative will not necessarily meet the demand. Thus, proposals to captive breed wildlife to reduce the pressure on wild populations do not necessarily lead to the protection of wildlife in the wild.

Final thoughts

Something must be done about the overexploitation of wildlife for food. Understanding that what motivates people to eat wildlife is grounded in preferences, necessity, status seeking and tradition may contribute to solutions to this problem. At the core of addressing this issue is challenging people's ongoing speciesist tendencies, whereby humans are prioritised above other species and humans' favourite species are prioritised above the rest of the planet's biodiversity. Of course, this a challenging undertaking, to fundamentally change humans' relationship to other species. With the rise of vegetarian, vegan and ethical diets, though, there is cause to be hopeful.

Note

[1] Bushmeat is the term used to describe meat that has been sourced from wildlife and illegally caught. The wildlife are often threatened or endangered (BCTF, 2009), rather than common species, which would likely be referred to as 'game'. The term is derived from the forests in Africa being known as 'the bush', but can also be applied in other regions (Asia and South America) (BCTF, 2009).

4

Wildlife for Sport

This chapter explores the killing and taking of wildlife in the name of sport via an examination of shooting, fisheries, game and poaching. As earlier chapters of this book illustrate, wildlife is often viewed as an exploitable resource and its status as 'property' determines the extent to which wildlife is protected (Wise, 2000). Most jurisdictions allow hunting of wildlife subject to regulation, which usually specifies which non-human animals can be killed or taken and which also places restrictions on *when* non-human animals can be killed or taken.[1] Regulations on hunting, shooting and fishing firmly relate to our wildlife criminology themes of commodification and exploitation and violence. The classification of wildlife as 'game' or as 'legitimate quarry' arguably commodifies non-human animals as undeserving of full protection from harm. In this context, wildlife arguably loses its intrinsic value and status as sentient beings subject to legal protection, and instead become something 'other'. In shooting and game operations, non-human animal life is in the hands of human hunters and game managers who are literally given the power of life and death over wildlife made available for sport activities. Our wildlife criminology theme of violence is also clearly in evidence in respect of activities whose aim is to end the life of non-human animals or which can involve deliberately inflicting pain on non-human animals. Such actions are, of course, frequently carried out with the sanction of the state, which will often derive revenues from hunting, shooting and fishing activities.

In discussing hunting, shooting and fishing within our wildlife criminology project our aim is not to directly challenge the legitimacy of these activities, although our green criminological lens would doubtless argue that the harms caused to wildlife through such activities are problematic. Hunting and shooting may not be problematic per se, given the necessity of shooting or non-human animal control in some wildlife or conservation management contexts. This is the case where non-lethal methods of control or translocation of a species might not be feasible and the presence of some non-human animals might even be harmful to other non-human animal species who require protection.[2] However, evidence suggests that legal sporting activities are inextricably linked to illegal activities and thus the scale of non-human exploitation and death is arguably much higher than what is recognised by official data collected by environmental, conservation or sporting agencies. This chapter examines the extent to which legal activities such as shooting and fishing are endemic with illegal activities including permit breaches, excessive catch, subverting of 'fair chase' rules and corruption within permit and licensing schemes. The chapter argues that the legal and the illegal exist side by side and thus problems within such regulated industries identify that offences against non-human animals are commonplace. This chapter also examines the poor regulation of non-human animal sports such that regulatory problems and inadequacies allow the continued exploitation of animals in a manner that legal systems fail to deal with adequately. This chapter also examines animal 'sports' such as bull-fighting which largely depend on violence towards animals and the spectacle of seeing an ostensibly 'wild' non-human animal 'competing' in activities alongside humans.

Sporting use of animals

Nurse (2013) identifies that traditional fieldsports are primarily focused on indigenous (native) wildlife where the original hunting activity was for subsistence needs, but which has now been appropriated for a social (sporting) countryside purpose, whether lawfully or unlawfully. The animal harm involved is frequently either some form of animal cruelty in the handling or dispatch of animals, or harm caused through failure to comply with regulations and industry practices that results in a failure to prevent animal harm.

A range of social fieldsports (hunting, shooting and fishing) are predominantly lawful although over the years a number of activities, such as hunting with dogs or animal baiting, have been criminalised by various jurisdictions yet continue as underground 'sports' despite the illegality of doing so (Kalof and Taylor, 2007; Smith, 2011). In addition, some traditional hunting activity exists in areas where hunting and its associated activities are carried out for subsistence purposes or have cultural importance (Nurse, 2017). In some cases, such activities also have a traditional social meaning where groups of rural dwellers participate in the activity as a social gathering. Nordic countries and some North American communities, for example, have a strong cultural history of hunting and gun ownership such that hunting large carnivores is seen as a culturally acceptable activity. However, where shooting is done unlawfully (that is, in contravention of regulations) it amounts to poaching, the illegal taking of wildlife or game animals for food, which is discussed later in this chapter.

However, the legality of some fieldsports-related activity does not negate the illegality inherent in or associated with some activities, which this chapter discusses.

Sport and trophy hunting are arguably separate from traditional subsistence hunting and are primarily motivated by dominion over rare species and also linked to the illegal trade in animal parts or derivatives such as ivory or rhino horn (Nurse, 2013; Wyatt, 2013a). Fieldsports as discussed within this chapter includes 'traditional' hunting, shooting and fishing practices carried out by countryside or rural community dwellers rather than the subsistence hunting of indigenous peoples carried out specifically as an integral part of their cultural identity (Preece, 1999). However, in addition to the (mainly British) definition of fieldsports as being country sports or blood sports, this definition also includes traditional hunting carried out by rural communities, which has a social connotation. Thus, for the purposes of our wildlife criminology discussion, the definition of traditional fieldsports used in this chapter includes game shooting in rural areas of the UK, the US and across Europe and both commercial and traditional (rather than recreational) fishing.

Eliason (2003) defined hunting as performing a traditional role, where the game taken is used and wastage is 'negatively sanctioned' (2003: 4). This definition identifies a fieldsport as being primarily based around the 'pursuit' of live quarry and representing a way of life where individuals kill animals primarily for the purpose of using them for food or fur (Brymer, 1991). Thus, hunters trap and kill animals in order to harvest their meat as food, or to use their fur for clothing and shelter, anglers catch fish primarily for food, and farmers and others (including animal breeders) may kill animals in order to protect livestock. However, our wildlife criminology project is primarily concerned with the recreational killing of wildlife which arguably cannot be justified on subsistence grounds. Instead it involves the killing of non-human animals for pleasure (broadly defined), which raises concerns about the commodification of wildlife and harm caused to non-human animals in the process. This also engages with our discussions of violence.

Hunting and shooting

Activities such as fox, stag and mink hunting (which were all until recently lawful in the UK) have developed from their perceived 'pest' control and wildlife management origins into leisure pursuits, as much about the sporting connotations of chasing live quarry with hounds as they are about population control of perceived pests (Nurse, 2013). Wildlife management differs from pest control because in theory wildlife management is concerned with maintaining healthy populations of wild mammals. Wildlife management models seek to ensure that wildlife population are maintained consistent with the local environment and allow for sustainable wildlife populations. However, wildlife management is largely anthropocentric and determines the overall balance of wildlife in terms of numbers that are acceptable to farming and other human interests in addition to considering the overall balance between different wildlife and livestock populations in an area. Thus, protected wildlife (including natural predators such as wolves) might be hunted or killed via 'pest control' measures where there is a perceived need to reduce or even eradicate an 'undesirable' wildlife population. The need to cull certain non-human animals such as deer is accepted as a conservation management technique, where non-human animals may have a negative impact on ecosystems or other human interests (Salvatori et al, 2002). However, the necessity to cull animals can align with economic interests where a possible surplus of non-human animals can provide opportunities for shooting and hunting to raise government revenues. Thus, trophy hunting in African and Asian countries is allowed primarily for economic reasons although conservation is also frequently advanced as a justification (Minin et al, 2016).

The economic argument reflects the reality that hunting and shooting revenues provide considerable benefit to the economy while allowing exploitation of natural resources. Identifying big game hunting as primarily an African concern, Nurse (2013: 155) noted, '23 African countries as having hunting industries with the largest in South Africa generating revenues of US$100 million a year (revenues paid to operators and taxidermists)'. Big game ranches, although perhaps not to this scale, also exist in other parts of the world. The conservation argument for hunting is primarily one of management – that hunted animals are those 'surplus' animals who would need to be culled in the absence of hunting, because their populations cannot be sustainably managed within their ecosystem and sustainable use is essential where resources are scarce (Baker, 1997). However, Lindsey et al (2006) suggest that there is a lack of consensus among conservationists as to whether trophy hunting represents a legitimate conservation tool in Africa. Hunting advocates stress that trophy hunting can create incentives for conservation where ecotourism is not possible. But Packer et al (2009) suggest that sport hunting is an inherently risky strategy for controlling predators as carnivore populations are difficult to monitor and some species show a propensity for infanticide that is exacerbated by removing adult males. In their analysis, Packer et al (2009) identified that simulation models predict population declines from even moderate levels of hunting in infanticidal species. The harvest data they analysed also suggest that African countries and US states with the highest intensity of sport hunting have shown the steepest population declines in African lions and cougars over the 25-year period prior to their study. Thus, at least in some cases, the efficacy of sport hunting can be called into question, where its conservation benefits and contribution to wildlife management are questionable.

It is undoubtedly true that commercial fishing (discussed later in the chapter) and game shooting industries can also be allied to food consumption and may make claims to providing healthy and nutritious alternatives to factory farmed and processed foods (BASC, 2011). However, sporting elements are also a significant factor in non-commercial hunting and fishing activities, where the challenge of pitting an individual's skills against those of live quarry, which can theoretically escape, are considered significant attractions of the sport as they are with trophy hunting (Lindsey et al 2012). However, this notion of 'fair chase' is questionable in some hunting contexts, particularly those of 'canned hunts' that involve semi-domesticated animals bred for shooting (Ireland, 2002; Hargreaves, 2010; Schroeder, 2018) or where management of non-human animals is such that the hunters are arguably at such an advantage that their targets are simply sitting ducks. Cohn and Linzey (2009) raise the question of whether involvement in hunting harms the hunters themselves. They point to the link between violence towards non-human animals and violence towards humans and the common link between murderers and hunters, especially murderers who dispatch their victims by shooting. While there is no clearly established, statistically significant link between hunting and either human violence or murder, their argument makes sense in respect of the possible escalation from one form of killing to another. It might also be explained in terms of the desensitising effects of killing non-human animals and the sense in which individuals may become used to the presence of death in their lives, especially where they have caused it. This issue is discussed further in Chapter 6.

From a green criminological perspective, the harm caused to hunted non-human animals raises various welfare concerns about the stress caused to animals in the hunting process as well as whether methods of killing are appropriately humane. For example, Bateson and Bradshaw (1997) studied 64 red deer who were subjected to hunting with hounds. Their analysis was the first scientific and observational analysis of red deer at the time of their death following hunting. Bateson and Bradshaw analysed blood and muscle samples taken immediately after death and compared these with similar samples taken from five non-hunted red deer who had been shot 'cleanly' with rifles. They concluded that the deer suffered as a result of being hunted and were not well-adapted by their evolutionary or individual history to cope with the level of activity (stress) imposed on them when hunted with hounds. In addition, they observed that 'the exertion associated with hunting with hounds resulted in marked physiological disturbances of red deer, including muscle damage and pronounced intravascular haemolysis [rupture or destruction of red blood cells]. We do not believe that these changes merely occurred at the end of the hunts' (Bateson and Bradshaw, 1997: 1713). The report provided the first evidence-based analysis that the physiological effects of hunts over even a relatively short distance and duration are severe for the hunted animal. Their analysis also concluded that longer hunts are characterised by signs of extreme exhaustion that would not naturally occur within short chases of red deer by natural predators, such as wolves (Bateson and Bradshaw, 1997). Accordingly, hunting was acknowledged to raise welfare concerns separate from any ethical concerns about the killing of animals and in response to the report the National Trust, one of Britain's largest landowners, banned the hunting of deer with hounds on its land (Mason, 1998).

Gavitt (1989), Hall (1992), Wilson et al (2007) and Nurse (2009, 2011) have all identified that wildlife law violations remain significant problems within the hunting, shooting and fishing industries. Where legal hunting exists, illegal hunting can often be found, in some cases as a form of open defiance against wildlife regulations that are seen to limit the 'right' to hunt. Von Essen and Nurse (2017: 377) identified that '[i]llegal hunting is undertaken by a wide swath of rationales across diverse cultural and offender profiles, ranging from the more prosaic drivers of thrill-seeking, trophy-hunting and ignorance of regulation to systemic socio-political drivers.' In some contexts, those involved in illegal hunting do so as a form of deliberate resistance intended to denunciate wildlife protection legislation, which is seen as illegitimate by communities with a commitment to hunting. Where such legislation is seen to criminalise a traditional customary or lifestyle practice, illegal hunting can become political and accepted within communities opposed to legislative wildlife protection (Holmes, 2007; Pohja-Mykrä and Kurki, 2014). Thus, hunters who illegally kill wildlife can become celebrated within their communities, avoiding social condemnation and law enforcement action. Von Essen and Allen (2015), investigating illegal wolf killing in Nordic countries, suggest that hunters publicise injustices through illegally killing wildlife, but the authors acknowledge that killing wolves as a means to deliberative ends disqualifies the hunters' dissent as legitimate disobedience, creating an obligation of deliberative uptake on the part of society. However, von Essen and Allen (2015: 213) also suggest that 'public authorities have a dialogical duty to provide deliberative uptake for the concerns of illegal hunters by offering them well-articulated explanations and justifications for new laws and directives', essentially a duty to better articulate the justifications for policies that have the effect of criminalising killing of wildlife.

From a criminological perspective this argument risks being problematic; from our perspective of wildlife criminology, doubly so. Acceptance of legislation is not a prerequisite for its legitimacy albeit there is a long discourse concerning the perceived fairness or otherwise of legislation. However, basic principles of the rule of law (Mackie, 1981; Raz, 2016) determine that citizens are not free to pick and choose the laws that they follow and as long as the law has been properly passed and the correct legislative process followed, citizens are expected to follow these as part of the social contract (Dunn, 2002). Arguably, legitimacy is derived from the use of the correct procedural mechanisms (for example, correct parliamentary procedure and/or the required public consultation) within a democratic society rather than the acceptance or otherwise of the legislation by particular interest groups. Von Essen and Allen (2015) raise valid and well-argued points about the perceived unfairness of wildlife protection legislation within hunting communities. However, similar debates exist in relation to the perceived unfairness of drug classification legislation, where mainstream law enforcement does not regularly allow latitude for those claiming a 'right' to consume prohibited drugs. From a wildlife criminology perspective, the notion of a right to hunt that provides a basis for ignoring legislation and perceived justification for non-human animal killings is problematic (Nurse, 2017).

Fisheries and fishing

Fishing (both recreational and commercial) raises concerns linked to our core wildlife criminology themes of commodification and exploitation, and violence, and we discuss these issues within this section. While in principle, commercial fisheries should operate on the basis of sustainable use of fish stocks, broad agreement exists that fish stocks are diminishing globally and that overfishing within commercial operations represents a significant problem (Watson et al, 2013). Commercial fishing operations thus represent a general problem in respect of resulting in a negative impact on wildlife by pushing some fish populations towards extinction. In addition, specific problems are caused where fish are captured and killed in commercial operations that utilise harmful or wasteful practices causing unnecessary deaths or using cruel methods to capture fish for food markets. In respect of recreational fishing, debates exist concerning whether this practice is harmful to fish and raises welfare concerns. This reflects issues around speciesism and 'othering' particularly in respect of arguments that dismiss notions of sentience among fish and challenge the idea that fish can feel or experience pain (Cooke and Sneddon, 2007).

High levels of fish mortality require consideration within our wildlife criminology discussion as the harm caused to the survival of fish species could result in extinction of some species within our lifetimes. Agnew et al (2009) suggest that illegal and unreported fishing contributes to overexploitation of fish stocks and is a hindrance to the recovery of fish populations and ecosystems. As with other areas of wildlife crime, statistical evidence of the scale of the problem varies and a precise, universally accepted figure on the scale of the illegal fishing problem is arguably not available. However, Agnew et al (2009: 4) state that 'lower and upper estimates of the total value of current illegal and unreported fishing losses worldwide are between $10 billion and $23.5 billion annually, representing between 11 and 26 million tonnes'. Flothmann et al (2010) identify that illegal, unreported and unregulated (IUU) fishing undermines sustainable fisheries management, particularly on the high seas (international waters beyond the jurisdiction of coastal states) and in coastal waters of developing countries, which has substantial social and economic ramifications.

Eighty per cent of the world's marine fish stocks are considered fully exploited or overexploited, leading not just to issues concerning species survival and welfare of fish, but also in respect of food security issues. In Global South countries where fish may form a larger part of the diet than in Global North countries, this has obvious consequences for poor and marginalised populations. It is also a particular concern for indigenous peoples who may lack alternative food sources or the resources to diversify their diet. Thus, sustainability in fish stocks is important for a range of issues. Petrossian (2015) identified that a country's risk of illegal fishing is positively related to the number of commercially significant species found within its territorial waters and its proximity to known ports of convenience. Petrossian's study of illegal fishing in 53 countries also concluded that countries that exercise effective fisheries management and have strong patrol surveillance capacity experience less illegal fishing activity within their territorial waters.

The welfare concerns of recreational fishing include concerns about the harm caused to fish in sporting activity, where the fish may be caught with barbed hooks before being weighed and released. Contemporary catch-and-release operations are intended to provide sustainable use of fish, allowing for them to be caught more than once in contrast to catch-and-landing fishing. Arlinghaus et al (2007) suggest that there are many ways in which recreational fishing stakeholders can modify standard practices to improve the welfare of fish, without questioning fishing as an activity per se. For example, fishers can choose 'fish friendly' fishing gear and handling techniques that minimise harm or stress to the fish to reduce welfare issues. Cooke and Sneddon (2007) argue that if carried out properly catch and release angling can be beneficial for the conservation of fish stocks, given that most of the fish who are released survive whereas fish caught by rod, line and barbed hook may well die even if released.

Growing recognition exists that fish can consciously experience nociception and have some capacity to experience pain and fear. Empirical anatomical, physiological and behavioural evidence arguably supports the notion that fish can experience pain and fear. Cooke and Sneddon (2007) suggest that numerous studies provide analyses of the consequences of catch-and-release on individual fish, demonstrating physical injury, sublethal alterations in behaviour, physiology or fitness, and mortality. Their conclusion is that all recreational fishing results in some level of injury and stress to an individual fish (Cooke and Sneddon, 2007). However, the severity of injury, magnitude of stress and potential for mortality varies extensively in response to a variety of factors. Davie and Kopf (2006) suggested that handling procedures used in recreational fishing need to match the environment where the fish are caught and the size and strength of the fish. They suggest that action that minimises the number of hooks on lures and baits and by using barbless hooks and circle hooks can generally reduce rates of injury and the severity of tissue trauma. A range of factors such as capture time, handling time and exposure to air play significant roles in the stress responses of fish and can arguably be minimised by anglers to reduce welfare problems and unnecessary stress. In addition, they recommend that keepnets, gaffs, landing nets, live wells and other restraining devices should only be used when necessary because each device can prolong or intensify the negative influences of catching fish by hook and line (Davie and Kopf, 2006). Thus, there is considerable scope to reduce the harmful impact on fish from a recreational practice that arguably does not sufficiently engage with welfare concerns. From our harm-based perspective, we would argue that if a sport is to routinely engage with wildlife-related non-human animal welfare concerns it should reorient itself and its practices in a manner that minimises pain and suffering to wildlife.

Game and poaching

Whereas hunting can be both legal and illegal, poaching by definition is the illegal hunting or capture of wildlife, usually infringing land use rights and game protection laws. Accordingly, poaching would arguably fall within mainstream criminology's consideration of crime and deviance, based on its position within a notion of theft of property. Von Essen et al (2014) argue that three main approaches have been used to frame illegal hunting and poaching: drivers of the deviance, profiling perpetrators and categorising the crime. Von Essen et al (2014) argue for a more integrative understanding that moves illegal hunting from being approached as a 'crime' or 'deviance' to being seen as a political phenomenon driven by the concepts of defiance and radicalisation. However, from our wildlife criminology perspective, poaching is problematic activity both in the context of being seen as more of a property crime than a crime against wildlife, and as being an activity that essentially shifts control and killing of wildlife from one 'owner' to another.

Humphreys (2010) identifies that significant ethical issues exist within the game industry. Most birds shot are raised in an approximation of factory-farming conditions, where considerable evidence exists showing that game birds endure extensive suffering in game production processes. While game rearing remains legal, the suffering that game birds endure in factory-type processes arguably identifies shooting such birds for sport as more morally problematic than other types of hunting and shooting. Gobush et al (2008) discuss the long-term harmful effects of poaching on wildlife. In assessing the impact of poaching on elephant populations, they observed that females from disrupted groups (that is, those where poaching had been an issue) had significantly lower reproductive output than females from intact groups, despite many being in their reproductive prime. These results suggest that long-term negative impacts from poaching of old, related matriarchs have persisted among adult female elephants for nearly two decades after the 1989 ivory ban was implemented. There are impacts on the surviving children of the poached elephants as well as we discuss in Chapter 5.

Poaching typifies attitudes of commodification and othering. The birds or non-human animals who are illegally taken and killed are simply there to be taken and in one sense are property that can be restored rather than wildlife to be protected. Eliason and Dodder (1999) in a study of the behaviour of illegal deer poaching in Colorado identified that neutralisation techniques were common. Four techniques showed up frequently within their study: the denial of responsibility, the metaphor of the ledger, the defence of necessity and the condemnation of the condemners. Thus, attitudes towards animal suffering as acceptable and justifiable are in evidence as is the case in direct sporting engagement with animals, which is covered in the next section.

Blood sports and exploitation of wildlife

Fieldsports, or blood sports as they are sometimes known, can involve pitting non-human animals against each other. Fox hunting, for example, was legal in the UK until 2005 with the introduction of the Hunting with Dogs Act 2004, which made it an offence to chase wild mammals with dogs. Hare coursing, which involves the pursuit of a hare by a pair of hunting dogs, often greyhounds, was a common pursuit in rural Ireland where Reid et al (2010) note that the speed and agility of greyhounds was tested by using a live hare as a lure. In hare coursing, live hares are taken from the wild and having been given a head start are chased by greyhounds with the result that some hares are mauled by the dogs, others suffer severe injuries and die at coursing events, and others suffer fear and stress commensurate with being chased by dogs and running for their lives. As Reid et al (2007: 427) note, '[t]he pursuit of game and pest animals with dogs is a common practice worldwide but is frequently contentious, particularly in terms of welfare and ethics.' Of note, the intention of hare coursing is arguably not to kill the hare. However, even where hares are not killed, the activity causes welfare issues and the accidental (although seemingly frequent) death of hares places the activity within wildlife criminology's exploration of violence against non-human animals. Hare coursing was only banned in Northern Ireland in August 2011 following the passing of the Wildlife and Natural Environment (Northern Ireland) Act 2011. Section 38 of this Act makes it an offence to participate or attend a hare coursing event or to nest or transport hares for the purpose of taking part in a hare coursing event. However, hare coursing remains legal in the Republic of Ireland and in other jurisdictions that may also allow other forms of blood sports, such as hunting with dogs or cock fighting.

Illegal fieldsports (for example, hare coursing) are dominated by gambling and distinctly masculine subcultures through which a hierarchy of offending is established and developed (Nurse, 2013). Illegal activity related to these activities is frequently an assertion of a particular form of social identity. As a result, despite legislation to control fieldsports in different parts of the world there remains resistance to law enforcement efforts, which are rooted in cultural and traditional explanations for these blood sports that attempt to retain such activities and their associated animal abuse in the face of perceived outsider threats (Nurse, 2013). Cohn and Linzey (2009: 317–18) suggest that the official classification of species as game (discussed further later) refers to 'specific species that somehow are incapable of suffering' or that any suffering involved is 'necessary'. But in the illegal fieldsports world, it is precisely the ability of certain non-human animals to withstand suffering and continue fighting (for example, fighting cocks or dogs and badgers) that identifies them as game or worthy participants in the 'sport'. Combative non-human animal sports are closely associated with illegal (that is, unregulated) forms of gambling, and criminal gangs involved in dog fighting, cock fighting and bear baiting are known to use cruelty in their training methods. It is known that the money involved in gambling is associated with violence and intimidation, which is used both to keep their activities secret and to maintain discipline within their networks. As a result, the police and non-governmental organisation (NGO) response to this combative animal harm employs many of the techniques used in the investigation of organised crime, such as surveillance and infiltration of the gangs (Saunders, 2001). Offenders involved in the exploitation of wildlife, farm animals or the rural environment within traditional fieldsports, as defined by this chapter, can commit their crimes for the following general reasons:

- profit or commercial gain
- thrill or sport
- necessity of obtaining food
- antipathy towards governmental and law enforcement bodies
- tradition and cultural reasons (Nurse, 2013: 123)

Our wildlife criminology project acknowledges that certain specific types of offending can only take place in rural areas as they are inherently reliant on countryside and wild species (for example, hare coursing, badger baiting, illegal fox hunting and bushmeat hunting) and represent a socially constructed form of non-human animal harm (Nurse, 2013).

Pitting humans against wildlife represents another type of sport designed to provide a spectator thrill at seeing humans risk injury, if not death, in combat with a 'savage' non-human animal. Activities such as rodeo riding involve the spectacle of man competing against animals as a test of endurance and skill. In one sense, bucking horses in rodeo represent wildlife needing to be 'tamed' or controlled, although realistically only a small proportion of horses will buck naturally, thus horses may need to be specially bred for rodeo purposes (Corey, 2011). Goldhawk et al (2016) in a study of 14 bucking stallions concluded that few stallions showed behavioural indicators related to fear prior to performance and that greater than half of the displays of escape or antagonistic behaviours by bucking stallions occurred at the same time as human activities that were not inherent to the rodeo performance. The Professional Rodeo Cowboys Association (PRCA, 2019) states that it has more than 60 rules to ensure the proper care and treatment of rodeo animals included in its official rules and regulations.[3] However, the Animal Law Resource Center (ALRC, 2014) argues that 'examples of inhumane devices that the PRCA claim to be acceptably humane are the electric prod, flank strap, and spurs'. The ALRC (2014) also notes that 'due to the violent nature of rodeo events, injury and death to the participants (both human and non-human animals) are not uncommon'. The ALRC (2014) describes practices such as 'the use of electric prods which cause intense pain to cows and horses, flank or bucking straps which wound and burn the skin, and the use of spurs to make the animals buck more violently. In addition, bucking often causes horses to break their backs and legs, which inevitably means death'.

These activities are of concern because they represent harm caused to non-human animals as an integral, albeit incidental, part of sport aimed at demonstrating human endurance in the face of (supposed) non-human animal aggression. Perhaps of more concern are those activities where harm to a non-human animal is the intent of the activity. Bullfighting, for example, involves professional performers (matadors or toreros in Spanish, toureiros in Portuguese, toreadors in French) engaged in close-range manoeuvres that are designed to force the bull into charging. The performer's skill is in evading these charges and completing a complex series of formal movements before killing the bull with a sword thrust.[4] Thus, Alamilla (2018) describes (Spanish) bullfighting as the ceremonial killing of a bull according to a formalized and traditional sequence of manoeuvers designed to display the skill and valor of the torero and the power and bravery of the bull, while at the same time taking advantage of the bull's fighting instincts to bring it into the position and condition in which it can be perfectly killed according to the rules of the art.

Arguably bullfighting is in contravention of European Union (EU) animal welfare laws (Nurse, 2019). However, it is allowed as part of the cultural heritage of Spain where it is a traditional practice, although one considered by NGOs, such as World Animal Protection and the International Fund for Animal Welfare as well as some academic commentators, to be non-compliant with good standards of non-human animal welfare (Odberg, 1992) or existing rules, such as the animal welfare laws of the EU (Nurse, 2019). Indeed, a 2010 ban on bullfighting introduced by the Catalonia Parliament was later overturned by Spain's Constitutional Court. The legislative change repealed an exception contained within Article 6 of Spain's Animal Protection Act 1988 by making bullfights and bull shows that include the death of the animal unlawful. However, bull dodging where the bulls were not killed remained legal. The ban came into effect on 1 January 2012. The Constitutional Court concluded that 'preservation of common cultural heritage' was the responsibility of the state and thus while a regional court could regulate a practice such as bullfighting that was deemed to be of cultural importance, it did not have the authority to ban it (Minder, 2016).

Re-examining wildlife and sport

As Chapter 1 identified, we consider both crime and harm as part of the wildlife criminology project. Some of the sporting uses of wildlife discussed in this chapter remain legal and thus would not fall within mainstream criminology's discussion of crime, except in those instances where illegal gambling or fraud are involved. But the legal is often associated with the illegal, in the form of non-compliance with non-human animal welfare and regulatory standards and the speciesist attitudes and practices that consider a certain level of non-human animal harm to be acceptable. As we set out in our initial definition of wildlife criminology, harm caused either directly or indirectly is problematic. Hunting and other sporting activities aimed at the killing or taking of wildlife cause considerable harm to non-human animals on an individual level where death or injury is caused and in respect of the negative impact on wildlife populations in a wider sense. The widespread existence of such harms indicates that current regulatory and legislative structures may be ineffectual. Furthermore, the prevalence of blood/fieldsports, indicates both wildlife's status as property and as 'other'. As we develop our wildlife criminology project, we encourage other criminologists to further examine the nature of such harms and the associated unlawful activity, to challenge the norms that underpin the suffering and harm.

Notes

[1] The process of 'closed seasons' in game and hunting laws denotes the period when the hunting, shooting or fishing of certain non-human animals is prohibited. Thus, some non-human animals may only be protected for part of the year and can be killed at other times.

[2] Wildlife management models frequently include measures that allow for the killing of some species (for example, so called 'pest' species) in order to conserve or protect other species. Wildlife and conservation legislation generally provides for this by specifying those species that can lawfully be killed in order to protect others. From our wildlife criminology perspective this is further evidence of commodification of wildlife and value judgements being made on which wildlife is worthy of protection and which is not.

[3] We note that while some rodeo non-human animals are specifically bred for the 'sport' wild mares may be used.

[4] There are, however, also 'bloodless' bullfights that arguably involve less bloodletting and animal harm (Dart, 2017).

5

Wildlife as Reflectors of Violence

Introduction

How many times have we all heard a human described like a non-human animal when they act aggressively or violently? This chapter examines the notion that human violence has its origins in the violence evident in our evolutionary history. The prevailing wisdom is that wildlife are themselves violent, and when humans act violently they are behaving like 'animals'. The exploration covers examples of violence by wildlife, including tribal 'war' between troupes of chimpanzees and rape by numerous non-human animals both inter- and intra- species. In contrast, the chapter also provides examples of altruism in wildlife, which counters the notion of human compassion as one of the exceptional characteristics setting us apart from the rest of the animal kingdom. The chapter aims to further challenge anthropocentric legislation by exemplifying common characteristics between wildlife and humans and in so doing set the scene for further exploration of the legal personhood of wildlife in Chapters 7 and 8.

Human violence stems from our animal origins

Animal violence is used to make inferences about human violence (Bradshaw et al, 2005). It is ironic, though, that people blame our non-human animal nature and/or origin for humans' violent behaviour. The irony comes from the (repeated) observation that humans are much more aggressive than other species of non-human animals (Georgiev et al, 2013). Georgiev et al (2013) speculate that humans' tendency for high levels of aggression and violence likely stems from an unusually high benefit-to-cost ratio resulting from such actions (that is, violence often leads to positive results in obtaining food, property, territory or 'mates'). They claim that their speculation about humans is supported by the frequent and widespread occurrence of killings of males by groups of males and of male to female sexual violence (Georgiev et al, 2013).

Yet, the notion that such violence stems from our non-human animal origin is engrained in many aspects of society. One of the founding principles of the discipline of criminology, though this is no longer accepted, is that criminals were people who were atavistic – the idea that such people retained some vestige of animal traits (Vasquez et al, 2014). People who were atavistic were seen to be more ape-like than human-like. The notion that humans who are violent are akin to non-human animals is persistent and fairly common, at least in English descriptions of violent incidents. In the course of their research, Vasquez et al (2014) found frequent usage of animalistic metaphors in media coverage, in particular, of violent crimes. The word 'brutal', often used to describe such incidents, has its etymology in reference to 'lower animals' (Koshy, 2013). It is argued that brutality is 'a vague generalization that was coined at a time when man was considered a special creation of God and divinely ordained to lord over beasts and fowl' (Koshy, 2013). While it is recognised that such language 'may constitute little more than a linguist flourish aimed at engaging the audience' (Vasquez et al, 2014: 337), interestingly and importantly, in such cases where animalist descriptions were used, Vasquez et al found a correlation to more severe punishments. They suggest that animalistic descriptions are linked to beliefs that the criminal cannot control his/her behaviour and that criminals give in to their passions like an animal would. This association likely influences people's judgements of criminal behaviour and the assumption that the criminal will continue to behave this way, thus deserving a harsher sentence (Vasquez et al, 2014).

That is not to say that non-human animals are not violent. Violence to control territory and to maintain or obtain natural resources is certainly a part of inter- and intra-species existence. It is difficult to see, though, how human violence in a mass majority of its manifestations is connected to these aspects. The difference seems to relate to the presence or absence of the intention to do harm and cause pain. Of course, this is likely an unanswerable question in terms of knowing whether or not a non-human animal intended to do something or not. In the next sections, we explore some examples of non-human animal violence to see whether we can discover more about the violence exhibited by non-humans and thus, humans, too.

Non-human animals are violent

Tribal 'war'

While violence is observed in probably all predator-prey interactions, there are some examples of violence outside these instances. In particular, chimpanzees have been observed engaging in violent conflicts between groups of chimpanzees and within groups of chimpanzees. Whereas some primatologists argue violence is frequent in chimpanzee societies (Gierstorfer, 2007), others propose that the amount of observed violence between groups remains small (Wilson et al, 2004). Kaburu et al (2013) states that the violence between groups is sometimes lethal and that such conflicts serve several purposes. If the instigators were to best the other group in the conflict, the winning group may have increased the area of their territory, increased their food supply and/or created a situation that will attract more females with whom to mate. The ongoing observations of violent encounters between chimpanzee groups support primatologists' beliefs that violence is a feature of chimpanzee society and that these conflicts are driven by access and control of resources (Wilson et al, 2004) These instances of inter-group violence seem to have justifications behind them rather than there being no intention, but, as mentioned, this cannot be claimed with certainty.

Much less common in chimpanzee societies, with only four documented observations, is lethal violence within groups, again between males (Kaburu et al, 2013). From decades of human observation of chimpanzee groups, it has been learned that male chimpanzees form coalitions and these relationships are crucial to the group's structure because they enable males to defend and/or advance their social rank within the group (Kaburu et al, 2013). It is then unclear why males within the same group would kill one another, since these coalitions are so important. In the cases that have been observed of lethal violence, the males who were killed were thought to be low-ranking males (Kaburu et al, 2013), which does not shed light as to the motivation for the killing.

The fact that chimpanzees form groups or coalitions made up of males in fairly large numbers does bear a recognisable similarity to human behaviour (Boesch et al, 2008). The conflict between groups over territory and the killing of individuals from opposing groups, also are not so dissimilar to human interactions (Wrangham and Wilson, 2004; Boesch et al, 2008). Furthermore, chimpanzees and humans seem to be motivated by both personal and group concern about status, and the desire to defend their group's integrity (Wrangham and Wilson, 2004). To do so, chimpanzees and humans engage in surprise attacks on other groups, have different subgroups composed of different members, and have not been observed all that often instigating entire group confrontations with their opponents (Wrangham and Wilson, 2004).

There are differences between chimpanzee and human groups as well. Wrangham and Wilson (2004) found that though chimpanzee groups and youth gangs of humans are similar, human youth gangs tend to be larger, the groups are made up of younger individuals than the chimpanzee male coalitions, the territories of human gangs are smaller, and human gangs seem to have a more complex organisational structure (Wrangham and Wilson, 2004). Human gangs also have to contend with larger human society outside the gang, which Wrangham and Wilson (2004) argue entails complicated interplay of cultural and environmental pressures that are absent from chimpanzee society. Clearly, the youth gangs in human societies are faced with challenges from individual and economic limitations, the police, their families and the social dynamics associated with criminal behaviour and (likely) being a racial minority (Wrangham and Wilson, 2004). These relations are governed in important ways by such factors as perceived economic and personal constraints, policing, family structure and levels of poverty, crime and racism. What Boesch et al (2008) suggest is different between the seemingly analogous behaviours in chimpanzees and humans, is that there are no recorded repeated peaceful interactions between males in the chimpanzee groups. In their extensive research of three habituated (accustomed to humans) chimpanzee groups in Taï National Park in Côte d'Ivoire, Boesch and colleagues witnessed killings of males between the groups for the first time. Interestingly, they did document peaceful behaviour between the groups, but only of female and infant chimpanzees. These interactions consisted of visits between groups of mothers with infants as well as year-long exchanges of adult females. These observations indicate that chimpanzee societies have further complexities than previously documented (Boesch et al, 2008). The size of the groups and the number of males may well be an important demographic factor affecting the interaction between groups of chimpanzees. The gendered nature of these interactions is another potentially important element.

This research is relevant to wildlife criminology in that it demonstrates the violence of other species that so often is thought to reflect human violence. In fact, Boesch and colleagues argue understanding chimpanzee society interactions allows for parallels to be made to primitive warfare and its evolution in human societies. Similarly, Wrangham and Wilson (2004), note how anthropologists and biologists utilise similar concepts in trying to explain the collective violence that is observed by coalitions of male chimpanzees and by human youth gangs. In both instances, the all-male groups engage in collective violence probably predominantly to achieve personal status, which is gained through physical violence (Wrangham and Wilson, 2004). A further interesting difference that comes out of this comparison is why some human males join gangs and engage in inter-group physical violence when others do not. In chimpanzee societies, what has been observed is that all males engage in coalition building and that coalition then participates in physical violence. Thus, Wrangham and Wilson (2004) posit that physical violence that is linked to obtaining individual status likely has different motivations in chimpanzees compared with human youth gangs. The value of understanding this difference is that knowledge about the causes of status seeking at the local level and how status gets achieved can serve as possible predictors of collective violence, when groups like gangs are formed (Wrangham and Wilson, 2004). Such knowledge has potential benefits when developing prevention and disruptions strategies related to youth gangs.

Chimpanzees are not the only non-human animal to engage in violence outside of a predator-prey interaction. And physical violence is not the only form of violence observed being committed by those other than humans. There are numerous examples of sexual violence being committed by a diversity of non-human animals, both against members of their own species and against member of other species.

Sexual violence

It will probably come as no surprise that many, particularly scientists, are hesitant to use the word 'rape' when describing non-human behaviours. The word rape is fraught with connotations of lack of consent, power and the intentions and motivations of the perpetrator, and it is difficult to ascribe such actions to non-humans when we clearly do not have a full understanding of what drives non-human behaviour. Instead of saying rape between or among non-human species, the phrases 'forced copulation' or 'sexual coercion' are used instead (de Bruyn et al, 2008). It is hard to see, though, when such 'forced copulation' is between species how this is not described as a rape, since the intention is likely not for procreation. The use of separate language provides further evidence of humans' speciesist tendencies and reluctance to use potentially anthropomorphic language when talking about non-humans. We, however, do employ the word rape in several of the following examples.

Rape, forced copulation or sexual coercion is a rarity among non-human animals (Koshy, 2013). Some possibly well-known examples are the praying mantis, ducks and geese. The motivation behind rape in these instances is thought to be the male forcibly obtaining access to a mate, likely when the normal mating rituals that he has performed have gone wrong or been rejected (Koshy, 2013). Thus, rape in these species is thought to have evolutionary underpinnings related to having offspring to pass along the genes of the males of the species. There are numerous other non-human animals who have been observed engaging in such actions. Palmer (1989) conducted a meta-review of the literature that recorded instances of non-human animal rape. He found that rape has been observed in insects, birds, fish, frogs, toads, lizards, acanthocephalan worms, elephant seals and non-human primates. Regarding the latter, rape has been documented in howler monkeys, chimpanzees, gorillas, and extensively in orang-utans (Palmer, 1989).

Rape in non-human primate societies and in dolphin societies seems to take place between groups, rather than within groups, though this is not always the case. For instance, the pods of bottlenose dolphins off Australia's western coast have been under observation for many years. Scientists have recorded that the male dolphins seem to form coalitions to protect the females in their group against males from other groups, who try to rape the females (Koshy, 2013). The anthropomorphic interpretation of this behaviour is that the male dolphins are acting chivalrously or gallantly in protecting the females. Evolutionary explanations of the actions, however, indicate that by protecting the female dolphins against rape by out-group males, the male dolphins in the same group ensure their own genes will be passed on. Supporting the latter theory was the observation that sometimes the male dolphins protecting the females would rape the female dolphins in their group, while supposedly acting as her defender (Koshy, 2013). Pinnipeds – seals, walruses and so forth – in particular, have aggressive sexual practices, where males frequently coerce the females to have sex (de Bruyn et al, 2008). Seals are also one of the first species observed to rape another species (McKie, 2012). Palmer (1989) notes that inter-species rapes between marine mammals clearly do not result in reproduction, and seem to happen in disrupted environments – environments that are degraded, have lost biodiversity and/or lost population numbers.

Antarctic fur seals were observed engaging in what the scientists thought to be abnormal sexual behaviour on the Terra Nova Antarctic expedition back in 1910 (McKie, 2012). The behaviour was, at the time, thought to be so disturbing that it was not made public. The notes of the observation were found much later and detailed 'the frequency of sexual activity, auto-erotic behaviour, and seemingly aberrant behaviour of young unpaired males and females, including necrophilia, sexual coercion, sexual and physical abuse of chicks and homosexual behaviour' (McKie, 2012). It was not only Scott and his team of scientists who have witnessed such behaviour. There have been four thoroughly recorded observations of Antarctic fur seals raping healthy adult king penguins during recent scientific studies in Antarctica (Haddad et al, 2015). The male Antarctic fur seals pin down an adult king penguin (it was not known if the penguins were male or female), the fur seals penises are visible, and in one instance, the rape was apparent because the cloaca of the king penguin was bleeding (Haddad et al, 2015). The scientists have speculated that rape of king penguins by fur seals may be a learned behaviour or possibly what they term 'displaced reproduction interference' because of an increased competition for females with whom to mate (Haddad et al, 2015). Antarctic fur seals are not the only non-human animal committing inter-species rape. Particularly violent incidents, with both rapes and killings, have been ongoing in several of South Africa's national parks.

Case study: elephant violence

Since the early 1990s, young male elephants were witnessed raping and killing rhinoceros in Pilanesberg National Park and the Hluhluwe-Umfolozi Game Reserve (now the Hluhluwe Imfolozi Park) in South Africa (Siebert, 2006). In 2001, it was reported that elephants were behaving violently towards rhinoceros and humans in several other reserves in the region as well (Siebert, 2006). The situation had become so threatening that in 2005 park officials in Pilanesberg National Park shot and killed three young male elephants, who had killed 63 rhinoceros in the park (Siebert, 2006). These particular elephants had also been attacking humans in safari vehicles travelling in the park. Whereas elephants in captivity are known to sometimes be aggressive, such behaviour in the wild is thought to be abnormal (Bradshaw et al, 2005). Scientists and officials were terming the behaviour 'violent' as there was clear intentionality in the actions (Siebert, 2006).

The violent behaviour of the young male elephants was not isolated to other species. Almost 90% of male elephant deaths in South Africa's Addo Elephant National Park during this timeframe were caused by other male elephants (Siebert, 2006). As a comparison, in more stable elephant communities it is thought that 6% of male elephant deaths can be attributed to other male elephants. There are a number of factors that scientists believe are contributing to elephants becoming violent to each other and to other species. Young male elephants who have just reached maturity have high levels of testosterone, which would at least in part account for the fact that it is young male elephants behaving violently (Siebert, 2006). In addition, elephants are known to behave aggressively to humans when there is competition between people and elephants for land and resources. These two factors are not out of the ordinary. What is new is the number of elephants, who have been killed by humans. Elephant societies are matriarchies where the older females – the allomothers – guide the groups. The number of allomothers and female caregivers has dramatically dropped due to poaching and culling (Siebert, 2006). Furthermore, also due to poaching and culling, the number of elder bulls has also dramatically dropped. The elder males in elephant society are the disciplinarians, making sure that younger males behave as expected (Siebert, 2006). This is particularly evident, since in some places the reintroduction of older male elephants with younger traumatised (which we expand on later) ones helps to quell their violent behaviours (Bradshaw et al, 2005). By humans killing elephants, we have completely disrupted elephant culture and society. Young elephants are not socialised properly, are in fractured groups and without key figures.

Furthermore, many baby and young elephants have been witnesses to extreme amounts of violence and are often the victims of trauma, as we alluded to earlier. These young elephants were present when their parents and the elders of their herd were killed (Siebert, 2006). It was common practice during the culling of elephants to leash the baby and young elephants to the bodies of the dead elephants until the babies and young could be moved to their new location (Siebert, 2006). Orphan elephants are known to engage in behaviour that is observed in humans suffering with post-traumatic stress disorder and other trauma-related disorders: abnormal startle response, unpredictable asocial behaviour, inattentive mothering and hyper aggression (Siebert, 2006). Evidence that the violence and trauma experienced by elephants is at least contributing, if not responsible for, their own violent behaviour is the fact that the adolescent elephants attacking the rhinoceros in the various places in South Africa, when they had been young elephants had witnessed the killing of their herd during culls (Siebert, 2006). According to Bradshaw, one of the leading elephant researchers, 'Elephants are suffering and behaving in the same ways that we recognize in ourselves as a result of violence' (Bradshaw cited in Siebert, 2006).

The examples here are just some of the ways in which non-human animals have been observed acting violently. Chimpanzees killing other chimpanzees in other groups or within their own group, the rape of another species, with clear evidence of injuries as in the Antarctic fur seal and the king penguin and so forth, all support claims that non-human animals are violent. Whereas there are similarities to human violence, as seen in chimpanzees in particular, a common theme running through the examples is that non-human animals behave abnormally or violently when their societies or habitats are disrupted. It seems likely, then, that the violence we see in other species is often because humans have been violent first, by killing their families or destroying their environment. Wildlife are more reflectors of human violence than vice versa.

Non-human animal altruism

While humans are not alone in our violent behaviour, nor are we alone in being altruistic and compassionate. Altruism, as with so many ideas, is a concept that has a contested definition. It is out of the scope of our discussion to wade in on the debate about what is altruism. We have adopted the definition put forward by Marshall-Pescini et al (2016) that altruism consists of 'helping' behaviours, which immediately cost the actor. The fact that the behaviours cost the actor but are beneficial to the recipient is why they are altruistic, rather than simply being prosocial. In addition, the actor is behaving alone, rather than engaging in costly behaviour as part of a group that is sharing the cost (Marshall-Pescini et al, 2016). Numerous experiments have been conducted to support or refute that non-humans behave in altruistic, prosocial or helping ways. While a majority of these have involved primates, corvids (the family of birds, including crows, ravens and magpies), grey parrots, rats and dogs have also been used as participants in these experiments. In each case, there is some indication that these non-human animals engage in behaviours that are costly to themselves and beneficial to others (see Marshall-Pescini et al, 2016 for more details).

Altruism experiments are most commonly designed to compare whether a non-human animal will share when another non-human animal does or does not share. For instance, common marmoset monkeys (*Callithrix jacchus*) in laboratories have been observed spontaneously giving food to other marmosets, who are not related to them and who have not given them food or do not reciprocate the giving of food (Burkart et al, 2007). The altruistic marmoset goes without food in order to give another marmoset, who does not have any food, their food. Burkhart et al (2007) speculate that since, like humans, common marmosets are cooperative breeders (many pairs of males and females having children without a hierarchy determining who can breed), so the sharing behaviour may stem from this societal structure. As other primates are not cooperative breeders and they have not been witnessed engaging in this kind of sharing behaviour, their hypothesis seems reasonable. However, primates have been seen collaborating in other ways. Female non-related bonobos cooperate to (violently) exclude aggressive males from their group. The suggestion is that females cooperate like this to maintain female dominance or to prevent infanticide common in some primate groups (we wonder, too, could it be to protect fellow females from rape) (Gierstorfer, 2007). As mentioned, similarly, bottlenose dolphins form smaller coalitions or alliances within their larger social groups (Simmonds, 2006). Not only do these alliances engage in cooperative hunting where different members have different roles while hunting, but these alliances also protect and control groups of females for mating.

It may surprise some that the non-human animals who are particularly altruistic are insects. Wilson (2008: 17) defines the behaviour as '[e]usociality, the care across generations of the offspring of a reproductive caste by a nonreproductive or less reproductive worker caste, is the most advanced level of social life in the insects.' Furthermore, 'eusociality requires collective altruism, which is behavior benefiting others at the cost of the lifetime production of offspring by the altruist' (Wilson, 2008: 17). Cooperative, social behaviours are so engrained in wasp and ants societies, in particular, that it is thought that '[s]ome wasps are thought to have evolved large eyes to observe social cues, and members of certain wasp species can learn the facial features of individual colony members' (Anderson, 2019).

It has been said, among many exclusive claims about human behaviour, that humans are the only species to die for their own species. Again, insects prove this belief to be incorrect.

> The new species is a member of the *Colobopsis cylindrica* (COCY) ... The COCY species group is known under its vernacular name 'exploding ants' for a unique behaviour: during territorial combat, workers of some species sacrifice themselves by rupturing their gaster and releasing sticky and irritant contents of their hypertrophied mandibular gland reservoirs to kill or repel rivals. (Laciny et al, 2018)

Furthermore, other species of ants have been recorded as sacrificing themselves to save their colonies; for example, a worker ant with a disease will remove himself from the colony (Rueppell et al, 2010). Similarly, Rueppell et al (2010) found that ill honey bees (which unfortunately were purposely given toxins or deprived of CO_2 in the experiment) committed altruistic suicide by disengaging from social functions and leaving the hive. Social insects then 'display altruistic food sharing, nest maintenance and self-sacrificial colony defence' (Rueppell et al, 2010).

Beyond altruism and cooperative behaviours, non–human animals also engage in other actions easily defined as positive or kind behaviours. Conflict in bonobo societies is usually resolved with sex, often homoerotic encounters between females (Gierstorfer, 2007). Whereas elephants engage in violence seemingly based on trauma, they are also known to display amazing forms of compassion and mourning that are usually characterised as exclusively human behaviours. Elephants mourn their dead, bury the bodies of their dead family and friends under bushes and soil, and visit the bones of these elephants for years – greeting them as they would if they were alive, by caressing their lower jaw with their trunks. It has been observed when an elephant has killed a human, they treat the human body the same way they do an elephant (Siebert, 2006). Elephants are not the only ones to apparently acknowledge their dead. Crows have been observed circling around other dead crows in what has been referred to as funerals or post-mortems (Anderson, 2019).

As with violence, altruism and/or cooperation are also not confined to inter-species interactions, as outlined here, but have been observed between species. It is likely that intra-species cooperation happens because both species benefit. Still, it is interesting to note that raptors, carnivores and predatory fish engage in cooperative actions (Clutton-Brock, 2009). In the case of the fish, groupers and eels form partnerships to scare prey out of coral reefs. It is believed that the two species coordinate their hunting through sophisticated head signals (Clutton-Brock, 2009). Of further interest, in this example, is the evidence of what is called theory of mind – an ability of an individual to speculate about the mental states of other beings (Anderson, 2019). In this instance, the grouper and the eel seem to know how the other will react to the situation. As we discuss in the next section, this further supports the lack of human exceptionalism.

The examples given here are from controlled experiments testing non-humans' responses to situations designed to display prosocial or helping behaviours or from scientists' observations recorded in peer-reviewed articles. There are, however, tens of thousands of stories from everyday people documenting non-humans acting in ways that do not appear to provide them with any direct benefit. Crows, for example, while they caw loudly at humans whom they seem to dislike, for people they do like, they sometimes leave shiny objects where the person can see what is apparently a gift (Anderson, 2019). The incidents of non-human animals behaving in selfless ways are often more dramatic. A brief foray into YouTube returns tens of thousands of videos showing non-humans saving or helping other non-humans, both inter-species (a lizard fighting off a snake who had a hold of another lizard) and intra-species (a hippopotamus pushing a baby zebra to the shore of a fast-moving river; a troop of baboons chasing off a leopard from an antelope; an orang-utan using a leaf to pull a drowning bird from a pond). Neither violence nor altruism are the purview of humans only.

Dismantling the exceptionalism of humans

As repeated numerous times throughout this chapter, humans have made a variety of claims as to how we are separate from the (non-human) animal kingdom. Criminologists, too, have made such blanket statements such as Brownmiller (1975) claiming that rape was only committed by humans. Other aspects of human society and existence that have been claimed to be exclusively our own are culture, morality and consciousness. It has now been observed though that other species' societies clearly have what can be considered culture. The earlier discussion of elephant graveyards and mourning is one such example. Culture is also found in cetaceans – whales, dolphins and porpoises – where social learning, including motor and vocal imitation, dialects, foraging specialisations, and different hierarchies and social systems between pods have all been recorded (Simmonds, 2006). And as with the elephants,

> [m]ost large whale populations were enormously reduced by commercial whaling (which peaked during the 1960s) but, whilst some recovery is apparent in certain areas, in some other traditionally important habitat areas there is none. It is therefore plausible that the whalers destroyed not just numerous individuals but also the cultural knowledge that they harbour relating to how to exploit certain habitats and areas. (Simmonds, 2006: 112)

It is often touted that humans are the only species with morals. For instance, '[h]uman cooperation is unparalleled in the animal world and rests on an altruistic concern for the welfare of genetically unrelated strangers' (Burkart et al, 2007). But as demonstrated earlier, behavioural biology and neuroscience are proving that this is not the case and that non-humans engage in 'moral' behaviours and react to inequity, which is linked to morality (Brosnan, 2011). Furthermore, non-human animals engage in

> reciprocity and food sharing, reconciliation, consolation, conflict intervention, and mediation, [which] are the very building blocks of moral systems in that they are based on and facilitate cohesion among individuals and reflect a concerted effort by community members to find shared solutions to social conflict. Furthermore, these methods of resource distribution and conflict resolution often require or make use of capacities for empathy, sympathy, and sometimes even community concern. (Flack and de Waal, 2000)

In addition to culture and morality, science has also come to embrace the reality that non-human animals, at least some of them, are conscious beings with emotions and able to feel pain and suffering (Anderson, 2019). 'Scientists are now finding evidence of an inner life in alien-seeming creatures that evolved on ever-more-distant limbs of life's tree' (Anderson, 2019). In the West, in particular, consciousness was part of the soul that was given only to humans by God. Interestingly, after Darwin's theory of evolution, while we blame(d) our violence on our non-human origins, it was still widely believed that the evolution of consciousness was a recent event (Anderson, 2019). Theories proposed that consciousness came into being sometime after the *Homo* ancestor split from our closest primate relatives, the chimpanzees and bonobos. Others argued consciousness evolved even later only with the development of language (Anderson, 2019). Such a stance to the non-human animal world was (and is) not apparent in Eastern philosophy. In fact, people like the Jains have been concerned with other species for thousands of years. They have 'taken animal consciousness seriously as a moral matter for nearly 3,000 years' (Anderson, 2019). The Jain religion is an Indian religion where other humans and non-human beings cannot be harmed. It goes so far in this aspect that there is no walking in puddles, as it disturbs the microbes, and no eating of root vegetables as this disturbs creatures living in the soil.

The belief by humans that non-human animals have culture, morality and consciousness has far-reaching implications for the relationship between them.

Final thoughts

We began the chapter discussing how wildlife are reflectors of violence in humans. In detailing examples of violence in non-human animals that may explain the origins of the violence exhibited by humans, it becomes clear that the violence in humans is most often very different to the violence by wildlife. It is most common for violent episodes by non-human animals to be driven by basic needs – reproduction, territory, resources. Intentional violence to cause harm or arising from trauma is the exception. It is arguable if the same could be said for human violence. The exceptional, intentional violence like the elephants killing and raping rhinoceros seems to stem from disruption and trauma that is caused by humans. If non-human animals respond to violence by becoming more violent, surely this has implications for human societies. We are evolutionarily linked to other species, but the connections we are focused on (we are violent because we evolved from non-human animals) are not evident when observing other species. It may be more apt to explore violence in wildlife reflecting their victimisation by humans as well as violence by humans culminating from their victimisation by other humans.

And while intentional violence may not be derived from our evolutionary links to the rest of the (non-human) animal kingdom, altruism and compassion may well be. Sacrificing resources and an individual's life are not exclusive to humans; non-human animals too engage in these altruistic actions. Humans are also not the only beings with culture, morals and consciousness; research continues to show people that non-human lives are much more complex than we have ever imagined.

What does violence, altruism, culture, morality and consciousness in beings other than humans mean for wildlife criminology? These are core aspects that challenge the status quo of who can be a victim. Human violence against wildlife is more serious than currently viewed with the addition of the destruction of culture and the harm against thousands of so-called lower species, like fish and insects, who are also altruistic, conscious beings. Human violence is also responsible for the intra-species violence stemming from our destruction of non-human animal habitats and societies. This, too, makes wildlife crime more urgent to solve than it is currently. In exploring how violence in wildlife contributes to our own violent nature, we have uncovered our responsibility to address our own violence against wildlife.

6

Wildlife and Interpersonal Violence

While not all wildlife crime involves violence or violent abuse, where it does occur it indicates that offenders may develop a tendency towards violence that manifests itself first in non-human animal abuse, but which sometimes escalates into interpersonal human violence frequently committed by adults against a range of victims (Nurse, 2009; Flynn, 2009). Violent activities involving wildlife may also indicate existing violent tendencies, serving as a means through which individuals can exercise their aggression or power-based behaviours. Wildlife crimes such as illegal hunting and trapping are violent acts that often result in the death or severe injury to non-human animals. The seriousness of the violence involved is sometimes dismissed by those involved via anthropocentric perspectives that view non-human animal life as less important than human life and use a range of neutralisation techniques (Sykes and Matza, 1957) to dismiss the problematic nature of much killing of non-human animals. Our wildlife criminology project is concerned with the extent to which violence inflicted on non-human animals is not only a problem in and of itself, but also may link to notions of violence in wider society. Criminological, theological and psychological discourse has also examined the extent to which abuse of non-human animals is linked to interpersonal violence (Linzey, 2009). Debates on this topic frequently identify that non-human animal abuse can be considered as a precursor to or indicator of later human violence.

Our wildlife criminology themes of violence and of speciesism and othering are explicit in discussions of the links between wildlife and interpersonal violence, which we explore in this chapter. We consider both general conceptions on the links between wildlife and interpersonal violence and the specific focus on the extent to which harm caused to wildlife may be an indicator of violent tendencies and possible predictor of future violence. Experts estimate that from 48% to 71% of battered women have non-human companion animals who have also been abused or killed and the link between domestic [non-human] animal abuse and human violence is widely recognised by scholars and law enforcement professionals (Linzey, 2009). Much of the literature in this area concerns the links between companion animal abuse and human violence and the notion that where one exists the other is also likely to occur. However, there are several different conceptions on the link between non-human animal abuse and human violence and this chapter focuses on one aspect of the link, that concerning wildlife and the extent to which wild non-human animal abuse can indicate a propensity or inclination towards other forms of violence.

Link between non-human animal abuse and human violence

The link between cruelty towards non-human animals and violent antisocial behaviour has gained acceptance within scientific and law enforcement communities. Within disciplines such as criminology and psychology, the link is actively researched with a view to identifying the causes of deviance and violent behaviour (Agnew, 1998; Arluke, 2006; Levin and Arluke, 2009; Linzey, 2009). For law enforcement, a basic correlation exists between those with a history of non-human animal abuse and those who commit serious interpersonal violence. The most common conception on this is the identification that most serial killers have a history of non-human animal abuse (Wright and Hensley, 2003); thus, law enforcement has explored the possibility that non-human animal abuse can be an indicator of future violent offending (Clawson, 2009). In addition, a number of studies have identified a causal link between non-human animal abuse and domestic abuse, concluding that in homes where domestic abuse takes place non-human animal abuse is often present (Ascione, 1993; Ascione and Weber, 1995; Lewchanin and Zimmerman, 2000). The relationship is a complex one and is not as straightforward as saying that an individual who abuses a spouse is also likely to be abusing non-human animals in the home. It can, however, be said that where an individual in a position of power within the family (that is, the dominant male) is abusing non-human animals, other forms of abuse such as spousal or child abuse are also *likely* to be occurring. Active or passive non-human animal harm in the form of cruelty towards non-human animals can be part of a cycle of abuse within the family or even a consequence of domestic abuse (although definitions of what constitutes domestic abuse are themselves not straightforward).

The knowledge of an apparent link between non-human animal abuse and human violence is not new. MacDonald (1963) identified three specific behavioural characteristics associated with sociopathic behaviour: (non-human) animal cruelty, obsession with fire starting and bedwetting (past age five). The MacDonald triad was instrumental in linking these characteristics to violent behaviours, particularly homicide, and in identifying cruelty to non-human animals as a *possible* indicator of future violent behaviour. Essentially, MacDonald linked poor impulse control, thrill seeking and an inclination towards violence and inflicting harm on others as traits shared by sociopathic offenders. Subsequent studies have confirmed that cruelty to non-human animals is a common behaviour in children and adolescents who grow up to become violent criminals (Felthouse and Kellert, 1987; Hutton, 1998). For our wildlife criminology project, we are concerned with whether those involved in harming non-human animals show tendencies towards violence that extend beyond harming non-human animals. But we are also concerned that violence towards non-human animals can serve as a gateway to other offending, but is not taken seriously because of the 'othering' of non-human animals as unworthy of criminal justice attention. The link between non-human animal abuse and human violence is inextricably linked to masculinities, noting that much domestic non-human animal abuse involving companion animals is caused by and a product of masculinities and power relationships within domestic relationships (Nurse, 2013). Children or partners, for example, can be manipulated into remaining with an abuser by means of the control exercised over companion animals (Browne, 1993; Arkow, 1996), while older family members can be intimidated into remaining silent about any abuse. Non-human animal abuse in domestic settings is thus sometimes a means to an end, determined in part by the vulnerability of non-human animals as powerless family members rather than their lack of any protective rights regime (Rollin, 2006; White, 2008). However, violence towards non-human animals can also link to abuse of non-human animals outside the home, such as stray or feral companion animals and smaller wildlife.

The abuse or mistreatment of non-human animals can occur for many reasons and can be either passive or active. *Passive* mistreatment can include neglect caused by 'failure to act' such that non-human animals (particularly companion animals) are not properly cared for and harm is caused either as a result of misunderstanding a non-human animal's needs or through deliberate neglect. Frasch (2000) identifies that beliefs play an important part in the treatment of non-human animals and understanding of their needs. *Active* animal harm consists of deliberate and intentional harm caused to animals (Daugherty, 2005). Active cruelty thus indicates some malicious intent on the part of the offender, which may be an indicator of psychological factors such as a predisposition towards cruelty (Ascione, 1993; Boat, 1995) and may also indicate that an abuser commits other forms of abuse within the home, such as spousal or child abuse (Schleuter, 1999; Turner, 2000). In respect of abuse committed against wildlife, this can be an indicator of other forms of offending. Those involved in illegal hare coursing, for example, are likely also to be involved in illegal gambling and may also be involved in crimes of violence related to intimidation of landowners and others who may seek to prevent their sport (BBC News, 2017; Bodkin, 2018). Thus, the wildlife crime (for example, hare coursing) is directly linked to violence in a manner that falls within our wildlife criminology project's broad concern with how abuse of wildlife links towards human violence. We contend that those who commit wildlife crimes and are prepared to use violence to do so should fall within the remit of mainstream criminology because they are violent offenders both in the sense of their (violent) harm to wildlife and because this is linked to other behaviours. The notion of acts such as hare coursing as lesser animal crime is problematic when human violence and intimidation are arguably inextricably linked (discussed in Chapter 4). Patterson-Kane and Piper (2009) indicate that acts of violence against human and non-human animals share commonalities. Wildlife criminology's themes of commodification and of violence provide a means to explore how violence to one species (non-human animals) may influence or cause violence to another. We are also concerned with the link between violence to, or inflicted on, wildlife and other forms of violence within society.

Non-human animal harm as indicator of violence

Linking non-human animal abuse and later interpersonal human violence is often explained via the progression thesis, which essentially argues that offenders start by abusing small non-human animals, progress onto abusing larger non-human animals and eventually escalate to human violence (Conboy-Hill, 2000). However, the strength and certainty of the link between non-human animal abuse and human violence requires cautious consideration. While the link is widely acknowledged and supported by the evidence of some research studies (Linzey, 2009), it must also be accepted that non-human animal abuse does not *automatically* escalate into violent behaviour towards humans. Non-human animal abuse is only one possible determining factor in later interpersonal violence. Many of the research studies that focus on non-human animal abuse and human violence also specifically examine the links between non-human animal abuse and domestic violence or violence within intimate family groups as this is a core concern of policy. Such evidence also discusses the link between non-human animal abuse and masculinities, arguing that much domestic non-human animal abuse involving companion animals is caused by and is a product of masculinities and power dynamics within domestic relationships. Accordingly, non-human animal abuse and domestic abuse, particularly spousal abuse, are arguably linked as part of a continuum of abuse directed by male figures towards more vulnerable members of their households (Nurse, 2016a: 1). Bell (2001), for example, identified that an increasing number of studies show that where adults are abusing non-human animals, they are also likely to be abusing their children. Non-human animal abuse within families, particularly abuse that involves inflicting physical harm on non-human animals, can thus be viewed as an indicator not only of domestic abuse perpetrated on partners and children typically by the adult male in the family, but also of psychological disorders that may show a propensity towards other forms of violence and antisocial behaviour. For our wildlife criminology project, we contend that this is also true of abuse and harm committed against wildlife.

Ascione (2009) identified that child maltreatment and interpersonal violence are significant factors in creating a wildlife offender. The evidence of the research is that individuals who come from homes where there is domestic violence and abuse of non-human animals are likely to go on to become violent themselves. The nature of that violence needs to be examined via empirical research, and for wildlife criminology we call for further research noting that not all such individuals will necessarily go on to harm non-human animals or become involved in the more violent types of wildlife crime (hare coursing, poisoning of birds of prey, badger baiting or shooting of endangered species). However, the nature of violent tendencies and violent behaviour towards non-human animals requires consideration as a potential threat to society, where such violence may escalate. Beetz (2009) suggests that abuse which affects empathy may be a primary factor in determining what type of offender an individual becomes. In particular, close relationships with non-human animals are thought to enhance empathy while violent attitudes towards non-human animals (and arguably a desire to kill wildlife) can indicate a lack of empathy. Cohn and Linzey's (2009) analysis of pigeon shoots in Pennsylvania, where schools are closed on the first day of hunting so that children can hunt, indicates that where children are taught from a relatively early age to kill non-human animals, this can become a part of their development that leads to a propensity towards violence and can escalate into other forms of violence. So too, a violent family environment, where children, spouses or non-human animals are abused, might damage the development of social and emotional abilities, which are said to be common weaknesses in non-human animal abusers (Brantley, 2007; Beetz, 2009).

McPhedran (2009) identified that cruelty to non-human animals often occurs with other violent behaviours, such as assault. As mentioned, cruelty to non-human animals can occur due to a compromised ability to experience feelings of empathy. Merz-Perez et al (2001) investigated whether violent offenders were significantly more likely than nonviolent offenders to have abused non-human animals of various types during childhood, examining cruelty to non-human animals categorised into four types (wild, farm, pet and stray). The results showed that violent offenders were significantly more likely than nonviolent offenders to have committed acts of cruelty toward pet animals as children. Henry (2004) researched the relationship between cruelty towards non-human animals and involvement in other forms of anti-social behaviour using a sample of self-reports of non-human animal cruelty behaviour and delinquent behaviour. He concluded that those who reported or engaged in or who reported observing cruelty towards non-human animals were also more likely to report greater involvement in a variety of delinquent behaviours both within the year prior to the study and over the course of their lives. While it must be noted that the study was of college students (and in the US, where a culture of gun ownership exists), who may yet to have grown out of any delinquent behaviour, the research went some way to indicating a link between cruelty towards non-human animals and other forms of criminal behaviour suggesting that young non-human animal abusers are also likely to be involved in other delinquent activity. Evidence shows that offenders who are engaged in activities for which there is a strong element of thrill seeking or 'sport' that involves the exploitation of non-human animals are frequently motivated by the power that they gain over non-human animals and justify their activities by denial of the pain caused to non-human animals (Sykes and Matza, 1957; Nurse, 2013).

For those in favour of fieldsports such as fox hunting, fishing, deer hunting or hare coursing, a common argument is that the non-human animal or mammal does not anticipate death and enjoys the chase. Evidence submitted to the Burns Inquiry on hunting with dogs (Burns et al, 2000) included arguments that 'the fox exists to pursue and be pursued' (the Morpeth Hunt) and that hunting with hounds not only 'destroys the weaker foxes it disperses the stronger ones' (the Curre Hunt) and so is a vital part of countryside life. The importance of controlling foxes as vermin is also emphasised as was the recreational and social aspects of hunting. Prior to the ban on hunting with dogs enacted in England and Wales by the Hunting Act 2004, the contention of hunting opponents was that hunting with dogs was morally wrong, but submissions to the Burns Inquiry from huntsmen, fox hunts, beagle associations and others emphasised the natural element of their activities and that they should not be subject to regulation. When the Act was passed, legal challenges to restrictions on hunting with dogs were made on human rights grounds, partially arguing that a right to hunt existed and that the restrictions were an unnecessary interference with a traditional activity (Nurse, 2017). While the challenges failed, they indicate the existence of anthropocentric attitudes that killing of animals is somehow a right that needs to be preserved (discussed further in Chapter 4).

However, in respect of our development of wildlife criminology, a broader conception on the link between non-human animal abuse and interpersonal violence is under consideration. Nurse (2016a: 5) suggests that if recognised in adults and considered within justice systems and social policy as more than just an animal welfare or animal law issue – that is, as a criminal act perpetrated on a vulnerable sentient being and as part of a continuum of offending – non-human animal abuse can be an important indicator of serious anti-social or violent criminal tendencies.

Wildlife crime and interpersonal violence

The reality of contemporary wildlife crime is one that sometimes incorporates violent activity. Büscher and Ramutsindela (2016) identify that over a thousand rhinos were killed in South Africa in 2013 and 2014 as the poaching crisis reached massive proportions. Evidence exists of an increasingly militarised approach to poaching in some areas such that the violence inflicted on non-human animals is both directly and indirectly the cause of human violence. The response to the African poaching crisis has been to use increasingly violent tactics to address poaching activity. This includes Botswana's 'shoot to kill' policy that targeted poachers through use of lethal force and was initially considered successful in reducing poaching activity and improving wildlife populations (Messer, 2010; Mogomotsi and Madigele, 2017). However, Lunstrum (2014, 2015) describes what is called green militarisation, involving the use of military and paramilitary personnel, training, technologies and partnerships, in the pursuit of conservation efforts. Arguably, as the commercial rewards of the wildlife trade increase partly through the increased rarity of wildlife products, and are linked to issues surrounding national security (corruption, sub-state insurgency and state legality), wildlife protection becomes increasingly militarised to combat the threat posed by armed poachers (Humphreys and Smith, 2011). Poachers who are often already armed in order to commit their offence may turn to violence against game wardens and others who stand in the way of their profit. Eliason's (2010) research into US game warden fatalities between 1886 and 2009 indicated that gunfire was the most frequent cause of death (36%) although when taken together, a range of environmental factors accounted for the majority of the deaths. Patten et al (2014) updating Eliason's research from data contained in the Officer Down website concluded that from 1886 to August 2012, there were 265 on-duty game warden deaths in the US. Their analysis identified that

> of the deaths, 113 (43 percent) were felonious, 160 (60 percent) occurred while the game warden participated in a fish and wildlife related activity, 112 (42 percent) happened in the Southern region and 63 (24 percent) transpired in the Midwest region, 96 (36 percent) occurred during the fall and 68 (26 percent) happened during the summer. (Patten et al, 2014: 33)

The changing nature of game warden duties is arguably a contributor to fatalities. Particularly in states rich with endangered species, the game warden role has arguably changed from one of nature conservation to one of law enforcement (Nurse, 2015; Eliason, 2016). However, unlike traditional rural policing, game wardens in areas vulnerable to wildlife trafficking may be more at risk of dealing with organised crime and violent armed offenders willing to commit violence or kill as part of their offending activity. Perhaps unsurprisingly, research suggests that attempting an arrest and rendering assistance are particularly dangerous situations for game wardens, and likely to incur assaults (Carter, 2004). Offender behaviour is also a strong factor in determining whether a game warden will be assaulted (Carter 2004; Eliason, 2006). Patten et al (2014: 38) noted a correlation between the largest hunting seasons (autumn and summer in the US) and the number of game warden deaths.

This discussion provides a snapshot of the context in which the growing militarisation of wildlife protection and of wildlife poaching activity links violence towards a non-human animal to human violence. In the commission of an offence, arguably those who have determined that killing a protected non-human animal through violence is acceptable may reach the same conclusion in respect of a game warden or other officer who stands in their way. The literature concerning militarised poaching identifies that violent altercations with poachers and armed militias risks becoming an escalating security problem and thus alternative tactics might need to be considered (Mabele, 2016). Lunstrum (2015) goes so far as to suggest that in South Africa, past military activity has been an enabling factor for current poaching – and that conservation-related militarised violence ultimately proves harmful to conservation efforts. For our wildlife criminology project, we raise concerns that a militarised approach may inevitably lead to an increase in violence, but we also contend that existing violence towards wildlife requires a full understanding of violent tendencies when developing policy responses to wildlife abuse.

While empirical evidence linking hunting activity with human violence is sparse, the drive to hunt and behaviours associated with hunting identify why hunting raises concerns. Elbert et al (2018) argue that intrinsic enjoyment of violence is a functional and non-pathological human characteristic. They suggest that there are essentially three types of aggression:

1. The Good: fighting to counter threat as a *reactive* defense
2. The Bad: *instrumental* aggression used to obtain social status or material goods
3. The Ugly: '*appetitive* aggression' which consists of intrinsic enjoyment of violence (Elbert et al, 2018: 135, emphasis in original)

Arguably, the latter type of aggression is involved in hunting and extreme acts of violence (for example, murder and massacres).

Elbert et al (2018) suggest that violence often results from a combination of these different forms of aggression; however, interplay between these types or an understanding of individual violence can be useful in determining how activities such as harming wildlife can lead to later human violence. If as Elbert et al (2018) suggest, 'appetitive' aggression is based on enjoyment of violence then such enjoyment may react to different stimuli and could change over time as individuals become used to particular types of violence. Hunting is undoubtedly an act of violence (Kheel, 1996), but the violence inherent in such activity is often neutralised by those involved in the activity. Flynn (2002) conducted a study to examine the relationship between hunting and illegal violence among college males. The study concluded that hunters were about twice as likely to have been violent toward non-human animals; however, the study determined that one type of violence – killing wild or stray animals – accounted for this difference. Flynn's study also concluded that hunters were more than twice as likely to have damaged or destroyed private or public property during their last year in high school, but were no more likely during that year to have fought with other persons. While it should be acknowledged that Flynn's sample was limited, a limited conclusion can be drawn that (for this sample at least) hunting related to harming non-human animals in the wild and to property damage, but not to other forms of non-human animal abuse or violence against humans.

Illegal hunters use a range of neutralisation techniques that involve rationalising their activities as not criminal and using various motivation-driven excuses and rationalisations (Rytterstedt 2016: 236; see also Eliason and Dodder, 1999). A complete list of possible neutralisations employed by wildlife offenders (as with some other offenders) can be outlined as follows:

• denial of responsibility
• denial of injury
• condemnation of the condemners
• appeal to higher loyalties
• defence of necessity
• denial of the necessity of the law
• claim of entitlement (Sykes and Matza, 1957; Enticott, 2011)

Different offenders may use different neutralisations and, may also be subject to different motivations. Eliason's (2003) assessment of poachers in Kentucky consisted of a mail survey to individuals cited and convicted for wildlife violations in Kentucky during 1999 with a follow-up survey to conservation officers in Kentucky during 2001. The second phase of his research consisted of in-depth interviews with offenders and conservation officers. Eliason's work identified that neutralisation techniques were often employed by those convicted of poaching offences. These techniques included denial of responsibility, claim of entitlement, denial of the necessity of the law, defence of necessity, and recreation and excitement – again, reflecting the research of Sykes and Matza (1957), which identified that individuals involved in crime use these techniques both before and after engaging in illegal activity. Significant numbers of those interviewed by Eliason were aware that they were contravening regulations, but considered that their breaches were minor or technical infringements and that they should not have been the subject of law enforcement attention. They often also denied the right of law enforcement officers to take action against them or contended that there were better uses of officers' time and that enforcement action should be directed towards the 'real' criminals. In addition, some offenders argued that it was necessary for them to kill wildlife in order to feed themselves or their families. However, our wildlife criminology project is not generally concerned with subsistence hunting and deliberate wildlife harm discussed within this book do not generally have subsistence needs as a justification for offending. However, we acknowledge that some game and poaching crimes have poaching for food as a motivator (for example, bushmeat), albeit our themes of commodification and of violence need to be taken into account.

Nurse (2011, 2013) identified that within wildlife crime a distinct type of offender exists: the 'masculinities offender' who is primarily motivated by power and notions of masculinity. Such offences are seldom committed by lone individuals. In some of these crimes, the main motivation is the exercise of power allied to sport or entertainment (discussed in Chapter 4); a link might also be made with organised crime and gambling. Such crimes, classed as crimes of masculinities, also include elements of cruelty or non-human animal abuse of the kind which is attracting the attention of law enforcement agencies in the US (Clawson, 2009). Examples include badger digging, badger baiting and cockfighting, as well as some crimes that involve the 'sport' killing or taking of wildlife (to be distinguished from legitimate predator control activity or, for example, the killing of badgers to prevent the spread of bovine tuberculosis). Research evidence suggests that in these crimes, the offender is likely to derive some pleasure from his offence and this is a primary motivator, and there is a link between some of these crimes and other crimes of masculinities (Nurse, 2013). Masculine stereotypes can be reinforced and developed through offending behaviour (Goodey, 1997) and are important factors in addressing offending behaviour which may sometimes be overlooked (Groombridge, 1998). The majority of wildlife offenders are male (Nurse, 2013), and in the case of the more violent forms of wildlife offender exhibit distinctly masculine characteristics. The literature in the UK and the public policy response are some way behind that of the US in identifying a group of mostly young males involved in crimes of violence (albeit towards non-human animals) that could turn to more serious forms of crime or expand their violent activities beyond non-human animals and towards humans (Ascione, 1993; Flynn, 2002; Clawson, 2009). Hare coursing, cock fighting and badger digging all involve gambling, with wagers being placed on individual non-human animals as to the outcome of a fight and other factors (including the power or strength of a non-human animal). For some, the associated gambling is as important as the exercise of power; significant sums are waged on fights, attracting the attention of organised crime. Offenders involved in these types of crime often rationalise, based on historical precedent or tradition. For example, Hawley (1993) observed that cockfighters often resort to argument 'based on pseudo-psychological notions: the birds feel no pain' and employ sophisticated arguments in denial of the pain caused. They are also especially aggressive towards non-governmental organisations like People for the Ethical Treatment of Animals and other advocacy groups whom they demonise as 'effete intellectuals and kooks' who lack understanding of their activity (Hawley, 1993: 166). The public policy response to masculinities crimes reflects acceptance of the propensity towards violence of offenders and is similar to that employed for organised crime. Techniques employed by enforcers include infiltration of gangs, surveillance activities and undercover operations. Masculinities offenders are considered to be more dangerous than other wildlife criminals and are treated accordingly (Nurse, 2011, 2013).

Olson (2002) identified that a common interpretive framework rhetorically informs different types of violent activity. She examined the discourse of sport hunters, 'hate criminals' and stranger rapists and concluded that in all three activities:

- rhetoric symbolically constructs and physically initiates an adversarial relationship with non-consenting victims/prey;
- victims/prey are selected opportunistically and constructed impersonally as relatively interchangeable class representatives;
- rhetorical devices are employed by offenders to distance and impersonalise victims/prey, without objectifying them or diminishing their presumed potency or the status accompanying conquering them; and
- offenders use rhetorical devices that express a desire to physically assert – and take pleasure in exhibiting – dominance and superior hierarchical status. (Olson, 2002)

Olson's findings link to our wildlife criminology theme of commodification and othering. However, in this context the victims are not seen as merely valueless objects, but are instead considered to be worth dominating. Within hunting, for example, certain species are considered to be particularly valuable and 'hunting safaris are usually sold in packages based on the key "Big 5" species; those which are the five most prized specimens for hunters; the rhino, the elephant, the leopard, the lion and the Cape buffalo. Some rarer antelope species are also prized by hunters' (Nurse, 2013: 156).

Non-human animal abuse and future violent offending

While much of the literature on non-human animal abuse and violent offending concerns domestic abuse involving companion animals, the link between non-human animal abuse and human violence is multidimensional, as is the link between non-human animal abuse and human violence incorporating spousal abuse, child abuse, elder abuse and escalation into wider (that is, non-domestic) forms of offending including serial killing. Bell (2001) identified that an increasing number of studies show that where adults are abusing non-human animals they are also likely to be abusing their children. But for our wildlife criminology project, we consider that we also need to consider the extent to which children who are abusing non-human animals are also likely to be victims of abuse themselves and the extent to which violence inflicted on wildlife and other animals may be a factor in other types of violence. This includes both where violence towards wildlife reflects a violent tendency that might escalate into human violence (such as the killing of game wardens and other professionals) or where violence inflicted on wildlife is an indicator of future violent behaviour and other forms of violence.

Non-human animal abuse within families, particularly abuse that involves inflicting physical harm on non-human animals, can thus be viewed as an indicator not only of domestic abuse perpetrated on partners and children typically by the adult male in the family, but also of psychological disorders that may show a propensity towards other forms of violence and anti-social behaviour. Non-human animal harm thus needs to be recognised not just as a factor in human violence, but as a form of abuse in its own right and as an indicator of antisocial behaviour or violent tendencies in both adults and children that may be associated with other forms of offending (Nurse, 2013). If recognised early in children, assessing the precise nature of childhood non-human animal abuse may be an important factor in diverting children away from future offending (Hutton, 1998) or determining the correct approach to deal with abusive relationships within the family. If recognised in adults and considered within justice systems and social policy as more than just a non-human animal welfare or non-human animal law issue – that is, (as we noted earlier) as a criminal act perpetrated on a vulnerable sentient being and as part of a continuum of offending, non-human animal abuse can be an important indicator of serious anti-social or violent criminal tendencies. Our wildlife criminology project argues that it is time for the link between non-human animal abuse and interpersonal violence to be recognised and acted on in all its forms.

7

Animal Rights and Wildlife Rights

Introduction

Earlier chapters of this book have clearly outlined that wildlife are victimised by people in a multitude of ways. As repeated throughout, we suggest that this is in part able to happen and engrained in most societies because of wildlife's status. Wildlife can either belong to 'no one' or belong to 'everyone'. They are likely the property of the state in either scenario. And, either way, their objectification – because of the speciesist nature of our society (Beirne, 2018) – enables them to be hunted or captured, usually within a set of regional or national regulations (Nurse, 2015). Once in the possession of an individual person, the wildlife shifts from being the property of the state to the property of that individual. Not all property, however, is equal. In particular, in many places the relationship between human and companion animals (who are also considered property) is governed by legislation that sets out guidelines for treatment of this kind of property and which often affords higher levels of protection to these non-human animals who are subject to direct human control. Similarly, 'livestock' or 'production' animals may be the subjects of welfare legislation that set out guidelines, which are likely less robust than those given to companion animals. Wildlife, who are outside the care of humans, may have some protection against hunting and trapping methods, which are deemed to cause suffering. Overall, however, even with welfare legislation, non-humans animals suffer and are exploited as we discuss in the next section.

In moving beyond the victimisation and exploitation that are perpetrated on wildlife, societies must create new relationships and legal structures to protect them. One way of approaching this is by granting some form of expanded rights for wildlife. We analyse how non-human animal rights are being expanded to include wildlife who are not companion animals. In this section, we include two case studies of legal cases in the US and Argentina, which are attempting to gain recognition for individual chimpanzees and orang-utans as legal persons, thus giving them rights. We critically consider these debates, arguing that under a lens of legal personhood, human exploitation of wildlife amounts to an infringement of certain rights. Finally, we argue for an extension of rights to wildlife in the form of legal personhood that protects them from certain forms of exploitation. To begin, we expand on why a rights framework is needed in the first place.

Why 'rights'?

There is a wealth of debate about non-human animal and wildlife rights that would be far too much to cover in a single chapter (for further reading see the References section). There are two aspects in particular that we will focus on here – the debate about improving and enforcing welfare legislation and the argument that certain protections are only given through a rights-based framework.

Welfare is not enough

Part of the debate about whether or not non-human animals should be given rights is why there needs to be a new approach rather than improving the existing legislation by better implementing or strengthening the law when it comes to non-human animal welfare. After all, the property status of non-human animals means there are laws in place outlining humane treatment and the prevention of unnecessary suffering (Francione, 1995). The question is, why is a rights framework or approach necessary when there are cruelty/welfare statutes already in place? As Francione (1995) rightly highlights, such legislation has and is failing to protect non-human animals in any significant way. We think one of the main reasons that welfare statutes are not enough is, as Tischler (1977) pointed out decades ago, welfare statutes tend to be reactive to punish people after the non-human animal has already been abused rather than proactive to protect wildlife from harm in the first instance. Furthermore, how can property (the wildlife) have recognised (welfare) interests that would outweigh the economic interests or autonomy of the owner? Francione (1995) argues that unless there is a human interest in a given context, non-human animal interests will not be recognised. In a system where capital is at the heart of decisions and status, it is difficult to see improvement for wildlife's welfare, should they remain property as it is currently conceptualised.

There are examples of non-human animal welfare legislation that make this point. In England and Wales, there is the Animal Welfare Act 2006. Under this legislation, non-humans are property and their owners have specific obligations to the non-human animal, in this case companion animals. The human must take into account the individual needs of their companion animal, which means the companion animal must be given 'a suitable environment, suitable diet, and the ability to exhibit normal behaviour patterns and to be protected from pain, suffering and disease' (Nurse, no date). What is immediately striking about the Act is that a great deal of the wording is open to interpretation and should require a fair amount of scientific underpinning. For instance, what is a suitable diet for a dog? Is the trend to feed dogs a vegan diet a violation of the Animal Welfare Act? Furthermore, whether or not we have enough information about the normal behaviour patterns of non-human animals is debatable and becomes more complex when taking into account the hundreds of years of domestication of companion animals and what role that has played in their behaviours. A strict interpretation of normal behaviours may well mean that spaying and neutering should not be allowed as procreation is a natural behaviour. We think not allowing spaying and neutering raises other welfare and harm issues if there were to be even more cats and dogs being born. In regards to being protected from pain, suffering and disease, this could presumably require regular flea and worm treatments for companion animals. In practice though, it is highly unlikely that someone is monitoring or could be put in place to monitor such actions.

That is not to say that legislation like the England and Wales Animal Welfare Act 2006 is not helpful or without purpose. Welfare legislation certainly seems to be a step in the right direction with regard to more recognition of companion animals' needs and goes beyond inclusion of suffering alone. In fact, Nurse and Ryland (2013) argue that the reframing of non-human animal protection through the Animal Welfare Act provides a form of rights for companion animals. The Act does so by requiring owners and other people responsible for non-human companions to consider the individual needs of their companion. Owners and 'responsible persons' are also required to ensure that the interior and exterior of their homes are suitable for the individual needs of their non-human companion, which is a significant change in English law (Nurse and Ryland, 2013). Other non-human animals under human care, though, are not afforded, *in practice*, this level of protection or recognition. Livestock, or deadstock as Beirne (2018) refers to them, are production animals, who, at least in Europe, are supposed to be protected by the 'five freedoms'. It is hard to see though how any industrialised farming of non-human animals could comply with these measures. In addition, it seems impossible that captive wildlife – in zoos, circuses, aquariums and so forth – are treated in ways which comply with the five freedoms (see our discussion in Chapter 2). The European Convention for the Protection of Animals kept for Farming Purposes[1] incorporates the five freedoms, which are a combination of animal welfare and protection measures. Again, these are:

1. Freedom from hunger and thirst
2. Freedom from discomfort
3. Freedom from pain, injury and disease
4. Freedom to express normal behaviour
5. Freedom from fear and distress

A brief exploration into the conditions of a vast majority of factory farms would reveal the environment does not provide for freedom from discomfort, whereas non-human animals have food and water. The same could be argued for facilities holding captive wildlife. Furthermore, factory farms and zoos are unlikely to provide enclosures where their captives are able to express the range of normal behaviours. The human carers try to prevent disease in livestock and captive wildlife, but captivity, crowded conditions, habitats filled with unnatural materials like metal and plastic, and slaughter clearly are not freedom from pain and injury, or freedom from fear and distress. Again, the five freedoms are a step in the right direction, but do not in reality alleviate much suffering or do enough to improve welfare.

Other European Conventions and European Union (EU) Council Directives also attempt to improve the lives of non-human animals. For instance, Article 3 of the Protection of Animals Convention requires certain conditions for keeping non-human animals. The article sets out that non-human animals differ based on their development, adaptation and domestication. Caring for a non-human animal must take into account these specific physiological and ethological needs in regards to housing, food and water (Favre, 2010). The knowledge underpinning the care regime should be grounded in scientific evidence and experience. We agree with Favre (2010) that this approach clearly indicates awareness of non-human animals' individuality as it does not establish generic guidelines across species with very different needs. The wording does not specifically discuss sentience, but seems to recognise non-human animals' capability to suffer (Favre, 2010). A limitation to all of the examples so far, as alluded to, is that by and large they only pertain to companion animals, livestock and captive wildlife rather than including 'free-born' (Sollund, 2019) wildlife. The notion of sentience is an important one to which we will return.

Another aspect of the welfare part of the non-human animal rights debate is as Garner (2013) notes, non-human animal welfare as a principle is widely accepted. Yet, we continue to witness alarming amounts of non-human animal abuse, because 'the moral inferiority of animals postulated can justify a great deal of animal exploitation. Such a position, therefore, is not, in practice, a reasonable balance between divergent moral positions' (Garner, 2013: 20). Furthermore, Garner (2013: 20) states, he does not think 'that the animal welfare ethic is morally permissible in the sense that it justifies inflicting suffering on animals provided that a significant benefit to humans accrues. This is to visit on animals a clear and fundamental injustice'. As property, as objects, even with legislation addressing non-human animals' welfare, wildlife are still the victims of human cruelty, because fundamental aspects that constitute a being's rights are not granted, cannot be granted, under such approaches.

The protection that comes with rights

Legal rights are essential for ensuring that the interests of non-human animals are taken into account in decision making during legal procedures (Favre, 2010). We advocate that non-human animal interests are not simply to not suffer, which is essentially, and not successfully, what non-human animal welfare legislation sets out to do. This leads us to Favre's (2010) three fundamental questions when considering legal protection for non-human animals.

First – directly to our assertion – do non-human animals have interests? As Favre (2010) states, this is a definitional issue. If thinking of legal interests, although non-human animals do not have the right to own or possess property, they certainly have an interest in using property or land to survive, find food, raise children and so forth. If thinking of interests in terms of bodily integrity, survival and flourishing, non-human animals, we argue, clearly have interests here too. However, Garner (2013) (also Galston, 1980) would disagree. He states,

> according to this position [enhanced sentience], which constitutes my preferred ideal theory of justice for animals, animals have a right not to have suffering inflicted upon them but not a right to life, since humans, all things being equal, have a greater interest in life. This does not mean, however, that animals have *no* interest in life. Consequently, most animal lives are of some moral importance, although

less than those of most humans. (Garner, 2013: 16, emphasis
in original)

Garner's proposed 'enhanced sentience position' is a rights-based
approach to improving the lives of non-human animals. He, too,
argues that rights are essential, or as he says, it is better to speak of
justice because this means there is a legal compulsion. Clearly though,
Garner's (2013) proposal prioritises humans over non-human animals,
which we suggest still leaves room for exploitation should the human
interest be weighed as being more important. But to reiterate, the
protection of interests – either considered equal to or less important
than human interests – can only be obtained with legal rights and
therefore access to the justice system.

Second, Favre (2010) asks do people understand enough about these
interests to embed them in legal systems. He poses that this question
is one of science. Are there data that provide evidence of non-human
animal interests? As we have shown in the previous chapters, there
is a wealth of information proving the emotional, physical and
psychological traits of non-human animals that supports their interests.
And such scientific evidence is growing by the day and required in new
legislation, as in the Protection of Animals Convention. For welfare
to be ensured and for legal recognition to be secured, we must carry
on collecting information about the interests (biological, social and
cultural needs) of wildlife.

Third, as a society, we must ask ourselves, do the interests of non-
human animals deserve to be acknowledged within our legal systems
(Favre, 2010)? Do the protections that only come with visibility by the
law apply to beings other than humans? The final question is, what
are our shared moral beliefs and how then do we express them in our
political and legal system (Favre, 2010)? Of course, this is the most
challenging aspect of a rights debate for non-human animals.

Steps towards rights for wildlife

Giving rights to non-humans is not out of the scope of reality. There
are numerous examples of where rights have been granted to people or
entities to protect their interests, which means that expanding rights to
non-humans is not only possible, but is already happening. Rights (and
justice; see Garner, 2013) are often associated with one's moral agency.
Several scholars argue that non-human animals lack moral agency, so
must be excluded from rights (contractarianism) (Rawls, 1971; Barry,
1989; Miller, 1999). There are several rejoinders to this assertion, but

a prominent one is that numerous humans also lack moral agency. Children and those who are mentally disabled, in particular, may not possess moral agency or always have the capacity to know their place in society. This is a key element of contractarianism, where 'parties to the contract are aware of their positions within society' (Garner, 2013: 8). Yet, clearly, this is not always the case and thus is not a reason to exclude non-humans. The same lens can be applied to corporations. Do corporations have moral agency and know their place in society? Only because the humans representing or embodying them understand these concepts. As Seymour (2004) states, the personification of corporations proves that the law is able to recognise non-humans, at least in particular circumstances. Many Western legal systems allow for guardians to be appointed for children and those who are mentally disabled. Corporations are also represented by a person. Should non-humans be granted rights, then courts would be required to recognise the interests of all parties (Seymour, 2004). The judge or jury would then weigh the different interests when making a decision (Seymour, 2004). In the case of non-human animals, one hurdle to overcome through this approach is who should represent their interests or act as their guardian? Is it the person who owns them, thus maintaining a property system for non-human animals, or some other person, who may be an expert (Seymour, 2004)? We will return to this in the case studies.

Such an approach that employs a human acting on behalf of a non-human raises the issue mentioned before – can the interests or rights of property be recognised? Favre (2005, 2010) proposes that this can be achieved through a formal recognition of a new category – that of living property. As part of being living property, non-human animals would be given their own 'equitable title' (Favre, 2005). This means the non-human animal has the right to obtain full ownership, in this case of themselves. What this allows for is a differentiation between living property and other property, which thus confers the non-human animal with legal rights and recognition (Favre, 2005). And as we stated earlier, legal rights are critical to being visible.

Within a new living property status, non-human animals would be protected from being held for or put to prohibited use, and from harm. What may be more radical is that under this new conceptualisation, non-human animals would have the right: to be cared for, to have living space, to be properly owned, to own property, to enter into contracts and to file tort claims (Favre, 2005). Clearly, such rights are much broader and more protective than the five freedoms (Favre, 2005). There are scholars who argue that an approach like living property, while likely to be better for non-human animals, does not go far enough to ensure the reduction or end of suffering and exploitation of wildlife.

Rawls (1971), in addition to saying non-human animals should be excluded from rights because they lack moral agency, also proposed that non-human animals should not be afforded rights because they do not contribute to society. Even if we were to take a very narrow view of society, there is ample evidence of how non-human animals contribute to it. Service animals, laboratory animals, non-human animals who work in human industries and non-human animals used in sport and entertainment clearly are part of the fabric of human communities. This list does not even include companion animals, which contribute in important though less instrumental ways. Furthermore, only considering non-human animals' contribution to human societies ignores the critical larger picture of how wildlife are crucial to the survival of humans. Without wildlife, ecosystems would collapse and so would human civilisation. Thus, 'not contributing' is a flimsy measure for not granting rights.

From sentience to legal personhood

While the concept of living property confers some rights to non-human animals, it remains an anthropocentric approach to other beings. There is little recognition of the intrinsic value of wildlife or of their sentience (though this may be beginning to change), which is closely linked to conceptualisations of personhood (which we return to in a moment). Just as immigrants, different races and ethnicities, and women were once viewed as less deserving of respect, the idea of non-human animals being worthy of respect is a natural progression of society (Francione, 1995). Other advocates for non-human animal rights offer multiple directions for obtaining protection for non-humans besides living property. We offer a brief synopsis of some of the more prominent suggestions before focusing on legal personhood and afterwards weighing in.

Singer's *Animal Liberation* ([1975] 1990) may well be the cornerstone of the start of the (non-human) animal rights movement. He draws from utilitarian principles and proposes that in order to achieve the greatest good, suffering must be reduced and there are no sound reasons to exclude non-human animals from this. Inclusion of non-human animals in efforts to alleviate suffering should not be based on perceptions of intelligence – after all there are humans with limited mental capacities – but simply on a non-human animal's ability to experience pain. Singer's stance is not a rights-based approach as such, since he rejects rights as a moral concept. He does, however, argue that all those able to feel pain should be protected from suffering. Interestingly, while Singer argues against speciesism, he still advocates that humans are different from other species. Similarly, in terms of humans being different from non-human animals, Morris (1998) proposes that people have an indirect duty to other species. In this approach, non-human animals do not have intrinsic value; instead, non-human animals should be protected because the interests of humans and non-humans intersect. Humans have an indirect duty to others with moral value, but not everything (everyone) with moral value has moral standing (Morris, 1998).

Drawing on her work in the economics of welfare, Nussbaum (2004, 2006) suggests a 'capabilities approach' to achieving justice (rather than rights) for non-human animals. Although in practice each of these will be expressed differently by different species, non-human animals should be entitled to life, bodily health, bodily integrity, play, sense/imagination/thought, emotion, practical reason, affiliation and control over one's environment. Humans have an obligation to ensure non-human animals can fulfil these above a certain threshold, otherwise an injustice has been committed (Nussbaum, 2006). Nussbaum's work, on both humans and non-humans, is grounded in notions of dignity. As we will see in more detail later, these capabilities are very similar to sentience.

Last, we will briefly highlight the approach of Francione (1995, 2000, 2008): abolition or species egalitarianism. He is the known for being more radical than other non-human animal rights scholars as his stance advocates that all species have equal moral standing. As such, although sentience (discussed later) also features in versions of abolitionism, no non-human animals should be used by humans. All beings have the right to not be treated as property.

In comparing these possible approaches, Garner (2013: 3–4) states:

> A valid ideal theory of justice for animals should also be rights-based, and should reject alternative approaches based on utilitarianism or capabilities. However, I do not endorse an abolitionist animal rights (or species-egalitarian) position that holds that, because animals have rights to life and liberty, it is illegitimate to use them irrespective of how they are used. Such a position is not simply dubious in terms of its validity at the level of ethics, but it also, it seems to me, requires so much of humans and is so far removed from the

current moral orthodoxy, that it does not qualify as a valid ideal theory of justice.

We, unlike Garner, do not suggest that non-human animals should be denied freedom from being used because it would be too restrictive for humans. Nor do we propose that efforts to give non-human animals justice should not be sought because this concept is too far from the current moral orthodoxy. We do, however, agree, at least in the short term, a middle ground needs to be found. In the longer term then, it may become possible to move towards species egalitarianism.

As evident from the foregoing highlights of the ongoing approaches to achieving better protection for wildlife, non-human animal (wildlife) rights debates often centre on the need to provide rights only for recognised sentient species, like other primates (chimpanzees, other great apes) and cetaceans (dolphins and so forth). Species considered to be sentient are widely thought to feel the range of emotions and sensations that people experience. Although the Convention on Animal Protection (discussed earlier) does not mention sentience, other European legislation does recognise sentience – Article 13, Treaty on the Functioning of the European Union. Under this legislation member states of the EU shall, since non-human animals are sentient beings, pay full regard to the welfare requirements of animals, while respecting the legislative or administrative provisions and customs of the member states relating in particular to religious rites, cultural traditions and regional heritage, when formulating and implementing the Union's agriculture, fisheries, transport, internal market, research and technological development and space policies (*Official Journal of the European Union*, 2012).

Singer ([1975] 1990) introduced that sentience is (should be) essentially the benchmark for personhood. Regan (1983) expanded on this by proposing the concept 'a-subject-of-life', which means not just being alive or conscious, but having beliefs, desires, perceptions, memory and a sense of the future. Being 'a-subject-of-life', or the components that make up being a subject, are one way in which sentience can be defined. Garner (2013) links sentience with a being's knowledge and awareness that they have gained or lost something. Another way to conceptualise sentience may be along the line that Beirne (2018) proposes, where emotions give the bearer the ability to initiate actions. Beings with the capability to act on these emotions have intrinsic or inherent value. Creatures with inherent value should never be exploited as a means to an end (Beirne, 2018). For Kymlicka (2017), all sentient non-human animals – domesticated or wild – should be given the universal right of personhood. This entails freedom from being killed, experimented on or enslaved. Beirne's conceptualisation obviously goes much farther than either Singer or Regan and would include many more, if not all, species. Presumably, this addresses the shortcomings of the previous proposals, which Beirne (2018) argues remain speciesist. Beirne (2018) rightly points out, such distinctions and gradations around sentience mean that the non-human animals with the strongest claim to personhood are those who are most like humans.

Wise (2010), the director of the Nonhuman Rights Project in the US, takes a slightly different approach in his efforts to obtain legal personhood for certain non-human animals. He argues that to gain legal standing an individual or a species must have the 'essential respects', which are brain structures, genes, cognitive abilities and levels of consciousness that are known to be correlated to sentience. The bar for obtaining legal personhood for Wise (2010), is for a being to have just one legal right.

There are other potential elements to legal personhood worthy of consideration. Legal personhood may also be linked to having a name or not because person-ness is tied to identity (Favre, 2010). Recognition in human societies as a 'person' could also be tied to the relationship the non-human animal has with the society (Francione, 1995). In the case of domestic non-human animals, they could be given membership rights as they are part of the shared community. Wildlife could be given different rights or a different type of personhood that gives them habitat and autonomy (Francione, 1995). In either case, non-human animals should be given the universal basic rights of personhood in addition to any other rights bestowed on them (Francione, 1995).

Even though there are variations on how to achieve or what may constitute legal personhood, in general it can be agreed that without the legal recognition of sentience, it is likely that animals/wildlife will, in jurisdictions where this is the case, continue to be regarded as things. In such instances, commodification of wildlife and thus their suffering and exploitation are likely to continue because status as a 'thing' means that that 'object' is property that can be bought and sold.

Case study 1

Non-Human Rights Project Inc. vs Lavery Appellate Court Hearing 518336

The chimpanzee, Tommy, has been kept in a cage in a room in a warehouse in Johnstown, New York, for many years. The

Non-Human Rights Project filed a case on his behalf (and two other captive chimpanzees) in December 2013, arguing that captivity is a violation of the rights he should be given. The supporting documents for the case included sworn statements from scientists about the self-awareness and autonomy of chimpanzees, which means they suffer living in a cage unable to engage in natural behaviours. Self-awareness and autonomy are key elements of sentience, which we mentioned earlier. The argument follows that because of their sentience and understanding, they are entitled to certain fundamental legal rights, which are given to 'legal persons' (Nurse, no date).

The Non-Human Rights Project asked for Tommy, and the other chimpanzees, to be granted the right to bodily liberty, which would mean moving them to a North American Primate Sanctuary Alliance sanctuary member or other sanctuary (Nurse, no date). While sanctuaries are clearly still captivity, they allow for as near to living in the wild as is reasonable and possible for chimpanzees who have been raised in captivity. "The uncontroverted facts demonstrate that chimpanzees possess the autonomy and self-determination that are supreme common law values that the writ of habeas corpus was constructed to protect. Both common law liberty and equality entitle him to common law *habeas corpus* personhood within the meaning of Article 70" (Wise cited in Nurse, no date).

Case study 2

Asociacion de Funcionarios y Abogados por los Derechos de los Animales y Otros Contra GCBA sobre Amparo EXPTE. A2174-2015/0 (Association of Officers and Lawyers for the Rights of Animals and Others Against GCBA (Government of the City of Buenos Aires) about Amparo)
In October 2015, a judge in Argentina recognised the orang-utan, Sandra, as a 'non-human person'. Justice Elena Amanda Liberatori ruled that the Government of the City of Buenos Aires and the Buenos Aires Zoo, where Sandra had been living for decades, had illegally and arbitrarily violated Sandra's right to freedom, her right to not suffer any physical or psychological harm, and her right to not be considered a thing or object (The Intimate Ape, 2015). This was after previous court cases, where Sandra's legal team tried to get Sandra a writ of habeas corpus, which would have given her rights similar to humans (Wise, 2015). The ruling of the appeals court means that Sandra must be found a home in a sanctuary that will preserve her cognitive abilities (The Intimate Ape, 2015). The process of finding

her a suitable home and assessment of her wellbeing is required to be carried out by an expert panel (The Intimate Ape, 2015).

The Buenos Aires Zoo closed in 2016, but rather than Sandra being transferred to a sanctuary as directed, the keepers of the renamed Eco Parque thought they could improve on the enclosure where Sandra lived (Calatrava, 2019). They argued that her life could be at risk in a sanctuary or if she were returned to the wild. Sandra did not, however, take an interest in the changes to her cage. In 2017, after reviewing possible sanctuaries for Sandra, Justice Liberatori chose the Florida facility – Center for Great Apes – which specialises in housing chimpanzees and orang-utans, who have lived in cages or been rescued from the illegal wildlife trade (Calatrava, 2019). Justice Liberatori chose this Center because of the large space, the similar climate to Buenos Aires and the possible interaction with other primates, which Sandra had been denied her whole life. Sandra first was flown to Kansas for a one-month quarantine (*The Guardian*, 2019). She arrived in the Florida sanctuary in November 2019 and was adjusting to her new surroundings as well as meeting other orang-utans for the first time in over a decade (*The Guardian*, 2019).

Neither of the court actions outlined in the two case studies was trying to get the great apes, who they were representing, regarded by the legal systems as being the same as humans. In both cases, there seems to be the notion that some rights given to people should also be given to sentient animals, especially apes, which humans are so close to on many levels. Classifying someone as a legal person or providing them with habeas corpus does not mean they are a human. But a legal determination of personhood would provide certain rights, such as the right to bodily liberty. Unfortunately, the state of New York did not find in favour of Tommy and the chimpanzees. Although there was promising language by the judge reviewing the appeal that clearly chimpanzees are not 'things', the ruling of the lower court to not grant habeas corpus was not overturned:

Does an intelligent nonhuman animal who thinks and plans and appreciates life as human beings do have the right to the protection of the law against arbitrary cruelties and enforced detentions visited on him or her? This is not merely a definitional question, but a deep dilemma of ethics and policy that demands our attention. To treat a chimpanzee as if he or she had no right to liberty protected by habeas corpus is to regard the chimpanzee as entirely lacking independent worth, as a mere resource for human use, a thing the value of which consists exclusively in its usefulness to others. Instead, we should consider whether a chimpanzee is an individual with inherent value who has the right to be treated with respect. (Honourable Eugene M. Fahey, Associate Judge of the New York Court of Appeals – Pallotta, 2018)

Legal personhood, probably particularly being granted habeas corpus, is a significant and, we argue, logical step for wildlife rights. Recognising that wildlife, even if at first it is only for a few species, have the right to liberty would provide an essential protection, which wildlife are currently lacking. We suggest legal personhood is the best way forward among the suggested avenues because there are numerous examples, mentioned earlier, where non-humans (corporations, rivers) are already considered to be legal persons. Legal personhood for primates also seems to us to be a possible stepping stone to eventually expand to more species and then more rights to all species. The fact there are dedicated organisations working towards gaining habeas corpus for specific wildlife individuals adds to the potential of the legal personhood approach to work because of the experience and expertise that has already been gained by their efforts. This approach seems to also be the best way to challenge the property status of wildlife and for them to no longer be considered an object or a thing.

Conclusion

Who then, as Beirne (2018) also asks, has the right to rights? 'What is clear is that the consensus in mainstream Western political thought is that the concept of justice is reserved for humans alone' (Garner, 2013: 5). In order to overcome this, as Garner (2013: 17) says 'it requires us to engage in a paradigmatic leap across the species divide jettisoning the anthropocentric culture that has dominated human social and political life'. Whereas Garner (2013) touts that this paradigmatic leap is not abolitionism, because it is an unrealistic utopia, we would not discount that species egalitarianism can be reached in the (very) long run. After all, as Farrelly (2007: 845) points out, 'there is some conceptual incoherence involved in saying "This is what justice involves, but there is no way it could be implemented."' Each case that advocates for an individual non-human animal, and each new discovery of the emotional lives and capabilities of other beings (non-human animals and plants) pushes human societies to take responsibility for the cruelty they are responsible for and to give rights to all.

The answer to who has the right to rights, therefore, continues to evolve. The answer will also depend on where one lives as different parts of the world and different cultures become more inclusive at different rates. By some benchmarks, for a being to be entitled to rights – able to fulfil duties to society, experience emotion and/or pain – not all humans would be entitled to rights (Beirne, 2018). This would be the case as well for the 'ability to reason' (Beirne, 2018). Clearly, placing some humans outside the right to rights is unacceptable and creates gaps for violations of humans' dignity, freedom from suffering and so forth. Such arguments for protecting all beings regardless of their physical and moral capacities, we (and others) suggest also encompasses other beings besides humans. The expansion of this moral circle (Singer, [1981] 2011), is ever widening as science uncovers more information about the emotional and physical lives of other beings.

We see two concerns with sentience as the metric for inclusion in the moral circle, though we acknowledge it is an important step in achieving justice for non-human animals. First, science has largely confirmed through various anatomical and physiological tests that mammals (and other classes of non-human animals) are sentient beings (Birch, 2017). This has not, however, improved the lives or reduced the suffering of billions of industrially farmed sheep, goats, cows and pigs. Sentience as a benchmark in legislation has also not ended laboratory experimentation on primates, mice and rats. Recognition of sentience has also not addressed the extensive use of non-human animals in the clothing and upholstery industries – fur, leather and wool. Yes, these examples are all governed by regulations and guidelines intended to minimise harm, but in practice, we argue, the lives of non-human animals remain full of pain and discomfort. Wildlife seem to receive even less protection. This appears to be supported by the condition of many zoos, aquariums and sanctuaries, and that the numbers of individual wildlife and species continue to decrease despite national legislation and international conventions to protect them. Second, using sentience as the metric for justice and/or rights excludes tens of thousands of species still assumed to be unable to feel pain or to have only instrumental value because they provide resources to humans. It is time to provide better protection for all our fellow Earth dwellers and as a first step, recognise that many or all of them are people too.

Note

1   The Convention is a Council of Europe measure rather than an EU measure. https://ec.europa.eu/food/sites/food/files/animals/docs/aw_european_ convention_protection_animals_en.pdf.

8

The Future of Wildlife Criminology

Are there only crimes against humanity (Derrida, 2002)? Certainly not. And wildlife criminology aims to expose the range of crimes against non-humans who are overlooked, ignored and hidden, and argues for an expansion of the criminological gaze to include harms against wildlife. This chapter examines the future of wildlife criminology in relation to each of the chapter topics to demonstrate the wealth of research that is possible, which can challenge the exploitation and suffering that is a fundamental feature of many aspects of our societies. We revisit wildlife as property, food (and other 'products'), sport, reflectors of violence and victims of human violence as well as their plight to achieve rights and justice. To start though, we return to a short discussion of language.

Improving our vocabulary

In relation to the themes of this book – commodification and exploitation, violence, rights, and speciesism and othering – the words and phrases used to detail each of these aspects, when talking or writing about non-human animals still, as we mentioned in Chapter 1, leave much to be desired. As a complementary project to the established critical and green fields of criminology, wildlife criminology can contribute to the debates as to what language we should be using as well as offer new terms that depart from the anthropocentric baggage of existing terms. What label can be proposed instead of 'non-human animal'? Can wildlife criminology help engrain the shift from using instrumental language when discussing wildlife, to language that reflects their victimhood – murder, theriocide, kidnap, enslave, rather than harvest, cull, capture, house. We hope that those who join the wildlife criminology project will employ sensitive language, whereby non-human animals are not 'it', 'something', 'pests', 'products' or 'commodities'. We should aid in making wildlife visible in any way we can and how we speak about them is one way in which we can give voice to their individuality and suffering.

Wildlife as property

Commodification and exploitation of wildlife, and violence towards them, are possible because of their status as property. Their status as property exists and the violence inflicted on them is possible because they are denied rights. They are denied rights largely because of the speciesist nature of societies. The four themes are so interlinked that they cannot be untangled and this is certainly the case with regard to wildlife as property. Yet, the notion that people can do whatever they like with their 'property' is undergoing a slow, but significant, change (but more significantly, is the change happening that sees wildlife are not property at all. We will discuss this more later in the section on wildlife rights). The case of Sandra, the orang-utan in Argentina, is a good example of this. She was the property of the zoo, but an Argentine advocacy organisation sued on her behalf so she could be given a better life. The ruling in 2015 found that the zoo must give up their property because they have violated her right to liberty. Sandra will get to spend the rest of her days in a sanctuary instead of in a cage. We suspect that Sandra will not be the only or last primate, mammal or non-human animal to be acknowledged in the courts and in society. Such recognition will not be confined to zoos. Legal challenges to free cetaceans from aquariums will also eventually be successful. In the longer term, it is plausible that zoos and aquariums as they currently exist will be phased out, and only those places that have high welfare standards, with 'exhibits' that are as near to the wild as possible, and that take care of rescued wildlife will remain. The role of wildlife criminology with regard to these changes in society is to expose the harms and crimes that are perpetrated in these environments. Wildlife criminology also seeks to expose the failure of legal and regulatory systems to address these crimes and harms. Empirical research on the nature and scale of the victimisation of the wildlife in captivity is a topic worthy of further exploration. Such data and theorising can contribute to the paradigm shift of wildlife as property.

Similarly, wildlife criminologists can contribute to investigating the plight of non-human animals in circuses and similar 'entertainment' venues. Here, we see a clear change in what society deems to be appropriate treatment of wildlife 'property'. For example, in the UK on 1 May 2019, the government introduced *The Wild Animals in Circuses Bill* (Defra, 2019). This legislation will ban the use of wild animals in England in travelling circuses. According to the UK government's Defra website, 'The use of wild animals in travelling circuses has no place in modern society and does nothing to further the conservation or our understanding of wild animals' (Defra, 2019). Animal rights charities have been campaigning for such a ban for some time. Dr Chris Draper, head of animal welfare and captivity at the Born Free Foundation, said:

> 'After years of waiting for this issue to be resolved, Born Free is delighted that Mr Gove [UK Secretary for the Environment] will now bring this Bill forward. The use of wild animals in travelling circuses is outdated and unpopular, and this legislation will bring England into line with a long and increasing list of countries which have banned this practice.' (Defra, 2019)

Dozens, if not hundreds, of wildlife held in captivity in these travelling circuses must presumably now be found new homes or be confined to some sort of enclosure, once in early 2020 they are no longer allowed to be forced to perform. It is significant that the government can force the owners to not use their wildlife property in specific ways. Wildlife criminologists and charities should monitor how this change comes about and examine how the new law is enforced and prosecuted. While clearly the legislation is a step in the right direction for non-human animal rights and the visibility of their suffering, there is the possibility that the implementation of the ban could cause unintended harms. What happens to the wildlife who are no longer part of the travelling circus? As stated, hopefully they are found new homes at sanctuaries and not confined to cages or murdered since they cannot be 'used' any more. Similar, unintended harms could appear in relation to wildlife as food as more wildlife are acknowledged as victims.

Wildlife as food (and other 'products')

Food is obviously one of the ways that a significant amount of wildlife is consumed. An angle to the food system, though, that has not been explored in any criminological research that we are aware of is the interconnected nature of the food chain and the knock-on effects of harms at any one point. For instance, the death of wildlife – bees in particular – due to exposure to pesticides and other human-made toxins, is likely to have devastating consequences on ecosystems, other wildlife and human food security. The speciesist nature of societies has meant that this form of violence has long gone ignored or unnoticed. The same can be said for (green) criminology, which too has a tendency to be speciesist, only focusing on the charismatic megafauna and overlooking the plight of other species. Where some research has been done on species other than cute mammals is with regard to illegal, unreported and unregulated (IUU) fishing (Petrossian et al, 2014). Here, mainstream anthropocentric frameworks – risky facilities – have been used to investigate IUU fishing. It is worth noting though that this research is not what we would consider wildlife criminology. The study, while valuable, does not argue for the rights or welfare of the fish (there is no concern for the fish apparent at all), but examines the human criminality and how it can be stopped through better regulation of ports. Examinations of wild food and the harms associated with their slaughter and the impacts of their loss on ecosystems are overdue.

Similarly, wildlife – particularly plants, though we do not discuss them in this book – are consumed in high quantities for medicine. Many cultures have traditional medicines sourced from the environment that date back centuries. For instance, traditional Asian medicines or traditional Chinese medicines have been used for nearly 5,000 years (Cameron et al, 2004). Likewise, in other parts of the world – parts of Africa and South Asia – non-human animal and plant material are ground up, dried or manufactured into plasters, pills or tablets. Bear bile, rhinoceros horn, saiga antlers, musk glands from musk deer, the teeth, bones and penises of tigers and leopards, shells of marine turtles, pangolin scales, Asiatic cobras, sea cucumbers and seahorses (Cameron et al, 2004) are just some of the non-human animals who are killed for their parts to become medicines or talismans against disease. This list comprises those non-human animals who are illegally hunted and traded for traditional medicines. The list would be much longer were we to include unprotected wildlife. Regardless of the illegality, many of the species in demand as ingredients in medicinal products are facing extinction, due in no small part to the traditional medicine market. For instance, the pangolin, who is becoming much more well-known, is hunted in alarming levels for their scales, which are used in traditional Asian medicines (Pantel and Anak, 2010). The scales are made of keratin, which is the same substance found in human fingernails and toenails (TRAFFIC, 2008). The four species of pangolin in East and Southeast Asia have been targeted by the tens of thousands (Pantel and Anak, 2010). As numbers in Asia have plummeted, the four species of pangolin in Africa have become the focus of poachers (Challender et al, 2014). The consumption of traditional medicines is a long held cultural belief. Part of this belief is that wildlife provide specific treatments and have special properties, but that the effectiveness of the medicine only exists or is best if sourced from wildlife rather than captive (or farmed) non-human animals (Drury, 2009). Thus, while there are non-human animals farmed for some traditional medicines (that is, tigers and bears), there remains a demand for wildlife kidnapped from their homes to be made into medicine. Again, the harm to the individual victims and to the environment as a whole is worthy of further examination.

Use of wildlife in medicines also needs to undergo (wildlife) criminological investigation because of the victimisation caused by the farming of wildlife for these medicines as well as unrelenting exploitation instigated by a cultural practice. For example, bears are farmed for their bile, which has a substance that helps to treat arthritis. First, the farming of bears causes a high level of suffering; bears are confined to small cages barely bigger than the bear, and the bile is extracted from their gall bladders while the bears are still alive, awake and un-anaesthetised (World Animal Protection, no date). Second, even though there is a synthetic medicine based on bear bile, bears continue to be subjected to this cruel farming. Finally, even though there are these (awful) bear farms, wild bears continue to be poached because the bile from a wild bear is deemed to be more potent. All of these elements of violence, speciesism and exploitation need to be challenged and form part of our wildlife criminology project.

We have not discussed at any length that in addition to food (or medicine), wildlife are products in other international markets. Wildlife are essential 'ingredients' and 'materials' of the fashion and pharmaceutical industries. While many of these materials for fashion (clothing and homeware) are taken from domesticated non-human animals, such as leather from cows, wool from sheep and fur from farmed animals like mink, a significant portion of leather, wool and fur comes from wildlife. Leather is sourced from kangaroos and from reptiles (see Arroyo-Quiroz and Wyatt, 2019, for the latter). Wildlife criminology could explore the harm and exploitation in these supply chains. The same could be said for wool from the range of camelid species, like the vicuna and alpaca, and the Tibetan antelope. Furs or skins come from a variety of wild species. Hares, foxes, coyotes, bears, felids, the list goes on and certainly depends on the location as to which non-human is trapped. The violence inherent in the trapping industry is another element largely overlooked (Wyatt, 2014) and wildlife criminology explores the extent to which legal activity results in or facilitates illegal activity. In regards to fur, while there were years where it was unpopular, somewhat recently fur has seemed to have a resurgence as a fabric of choice. In response, there are several places around the world that are banning fur altogether (Kapner, 2019), which bodes well for the non-human animals.

Wildlife as sport

Hunting, in general, and trophy hunting, in particular, are aspects of human–wildlife interaction that are taken for granted as being cultural, traditional entitlements and practices, but – like circuses and zoos – need to be re-examined. The practice of hunting itself, which obviously ties into discussions of the ethics of meat eating and dairy consumption, is worthy of criminological exploration because it contains each of the four themes we have presented in this book – commodification and exploitation, violence, rights, and speciesism and othering. Grouse hunting in England is a good example of how each theme intertwines with the other. To shoot a wild grouse, people (mostly men) pay £75 per bird. Grouse hunting is highly controlled, and the grouse are driven out of the heather by people known as 'beaters' on the moors of northern England (Avery, 2017). These moors are intensively managed to enable the grouse to flourish. Wetlands are drained to make more moorland, fires are set to clear out vegetation besides heather, and all other wildlife who either would eat the grouse (foxes, birds of prey) or eat what the grouse eat (hares) are killed (Avery, 2017). There are so many grouse being born and raised in crowded conditions that they are given medication to prevent diseases. By the end of the 16-week grouse-hunting season, around 500,000 grouse have been killed (Avery, 2017). It is unlikely that all of the grouse are eaten; most of them probably are discarded. The grouse are a commodity. The moorlands are exploited to accommodate this commodity at the expense of a healthy environment and the lives of other wildlife. Grouse, because they have value to humans, are prioritised above other species in a clear example of speciesism. The scale of death we suggest is clear evidence of the violence involved. How is this not an injustice? Or a violation of the rights of the many victims?

The structure of the grouse hunting industry is one of several ways in which 'sport' hunting is managed. As we discussed in Chapter 4, canned or trophy hunting expeditions have other approaches. In hunting in general, certain species are singled out for intrusive management operations to ensure non-human animals will be available for humans to kill. In many of these industries, there is arguably very little 'sport' or skill involved. In grouse hunts, there are hundreds if not thousands of birds flushed out from the heather for people to take aim at. It is probably uncommon for someone to go home empty handed.

Hunting may be the most intractable form of sport remaining in human societies. Other so-called sports – various non-human animals fighting each other or people, baiting activities and so forth – while still in existence, seem to be much less prevalent and often prohibited by law. That is not to say these topics are not worthy of further study; indeed, they are. The dynamics and consequences of these forms of violence against non-human animals still have much to teach us about the nature of human violence.

Wildlife as reflectors of violence and the target of human violence

In Chapter 5, we gave examples of where non-human animals are violent and how that is said to reflect why humans are violent. In Chapter 6, we analysed the evidence that links the violence inflicted on non-human animals by humans, possibly leading to humans acting violently towards one another. What emerged from these discussions is that the violence perpetrated on wildlife and between humans is a complex phenomenon that warrants continued research and greater consideration by legal systems and policy. The analysis of instances of intra- and inter-species violence uncovered that the environment in which non-human animals are forced to live is one permeated with violence and that exposure may well be correlated to their own violent behaviour. The human damage to non-human animal cultures is a topic in need of investigation. On the flip side, it is likely true as well, that in some cases humans who are exposed to violence against non-human animals could be desensitised to violence and then become more aggressive and violent. The link between the commission of violent acts like non-human abuse and cruelty and engaging in violent acts to humans is fairly well established (Conboy-Hill, 2000; Linzey, 2009). What has yet to be determined is whether not just commission of violence, but *exposure* to violence also plays a part in making people more violent than they otherwise might be. As part of research in this area, wildlife criminologists may choose to investigate and challenge the definitions of violence itself. Is eating meat a form of violence? Is hunting? Clearly, there are arguments for and against including these behaviours in conceptualisations of violence. It is important to unpack whether being surrounded by subtle beneath-the-surface reminders of death and suffering (our food, clothing and so forth) somehow tie into the violence that humans perpetrate.

Wildlife rights

As we detailed in Chapter 7, there are numerous ways in which non-human animal rights advocates and scholars are proposing how protections for wildlife can be improved. We concur with many of them that improvements to welfare statutes are limited in effectiveness. More importantly, only addressing legislation about welfare sends the message and perpetuates the status quo that non-human animals are property. Yes, we should take better care of our property, but this is the very paradigm shift that we need to be striving for if we are truly to alleviate human-caused suffering of other species. In the current context, we think the efforts to get recognition for some individual non-human animals as legal persons shows the most promise. We predict that the Nonhuman Rights Project will win one of its cases – be it for Tommy or another chimpanzee or the other cases they have filed to have captive elephants recognised as legal persons.

As repeated several times, without rights, non-human animals do not have access to or a voice in the justice system. They also do not have a voice in decision making and environmental governance. This absence is in desperate need of attention, particularly with the impending hard decisions that must be made in light of climate change. Non-human animals are already being affected by the changes to the climate. The heart-breaking pictures of starving polar bears unable to find food because of the lack of ice is one of many examples. As governments and communities derive and implement adaptation and mitigation strategies, who is speaking for the non-human animals? Debates are already being had as to which among the species scientists should try to save. What is being called 'managed relocation' or 'assisted migration' will be critical for the survival of some species (Early and Fax, 2011). Species who are unable to adapt quickly enough to the effects of climate change and who are incapable of migrating will need human assistance to survive (Borrell, 2009; Early and Fax, 2011). There are several reasons that this is controversial. Should humans be intervening at all? The motivations behind saving non-human animals is admirable, but it is possible that the unintended consequences and harms will make this approach inadvisable. The complexity and costs of capturing and moving entire populations of species are daunting. We probably cannot accurately predict the consequences to the ecosystems where species are moved from and even less likely to know the consequences to the ecosystems where species are moved to. A key part of the controversy, though, is how and who will determine which species are moved.

The decision about who will be saved and who will not is likely to be rife with speciesism. This is despite the formula scientists are devising to prioritise which species to move and where to move them to (Milman, 2013). This formula reports that this formula will be calculated based on the status of the non-human animals to be moved (endangered, threatened and so forth), the prospect for survival of the non-human animals at their new locations, and the impact of the relocated non-human animals on the existing species in the new areas Milman (2013). Each of these categories is determined through the lens of human knowledge. There is so much that is unknown and so much speculation about the exact numbers of species, how the alien or invasive species will fare in their new habitats, and what the implications are for those ecosystems. The human voice is the only voice deciding where suitable new homes for species are and which species get homes at all. Such a process is riddled with anthropocentric value judgements and human hubris about how much is known about and manageable in the environment, and who is worth saving.

Expanding the circle

A majority of the time, the theriocide of non-human animals is invisible and legal (Beirne, 2018). Wildlife criminology, like green criminology, is not confined by the crafted definitions of crimes against wildlife by the powerful or the state. Wildlife criminology seeks to expose theriocide and other violence against non-human animals regardless of its legality or illegality. We also endeavour to, in Singer's ([1981] 2011) words, expand the circle by not just analysing and researching the harms and crimes against mammals and charismatic megafauna, but to also encourage and support critical engagement with the violence and victimisation perpetrated against *all* non-human animals. We hope that the examples that have underpinned our discussions in this (first) book have made some strides in that direction.

The expansion of the circle should not, however, end there. In the future, wildlife criminology will not just address non-human animals. There is much work to be done to speak out for and protect plants and fungi against the devastation wrought on them by humans. As scientific studies are showing us, plants may well not be the passive objects we have thought that they were (Trewavas, 2003; Chamovitz, 2013). A wealth of scientific studies evidence that trees of the same species are communal and that trees of different species form alliances (Grant, 2018). Vast fungal underground networks intertwined with the roots of the trees enable trees to share water and communicate

(Wohlleben, 2016). Through sending chemical, hormonal and slow-pulsing electrical signals along these networks, trees warn each other of drought, disease and insect invasions, and those receiving the messages are known to respond (Wohlleben, 2016). Scientists are just beginning to understand some of the trees' communication and have only recently discovered the emission and detection of sounds occurring between trees (Grant, 2018). Communication is not limited to sound or the underground network. Trees also transmit and receive pheromones and other scent signals through the air, not unlike a sense of smell (Wohlleben, 2016). The fact that trees respond differently to a human hand breaking a branch and a deer chewing that same branch has led scientists to postulate trees also have a sense of 'taste' since their chemical response is in response to the deer's saliva (Grant, 2018). Data also point to forests having 'mother' trees; saplings who are not receiving enough sunlight to photosynthesise properly, and tree stumps from trees that have been cut down, sometimes hundreds of years ago, survive when, at least above ground, there is no visible reason that they should (Wohlleben, 2016). The great matriarchs of the tree communities share their resources with the saplings and the stumps, thereby ensuring their survival (Grant, 2018). Such knowledge is revolutionary and has the potential to radically alter our relationship with trees and other plants. It completely altered the way that Wohlleben (2016), a forester by occupation, came to manage forests. After he came to understand the fungal networks, he employed less-invasive logging techniques, which kept these networks intact where possible (Grant, 2018). The result: healthier forests with bigger trees.

We are coming to know that trees and plants, in addition to other animals, are communicating and helping each other. This information makes a strong case for expanding the circle of rights and justice to include many more species. How far should the circle go? While we may wish for all life to be included in considerations to prevent harm and suffering, we do realise this is in the very distant future were it to happen at all. With climate change upon us and with the ongoing sixth mass extinction (IPBES, 2019), the circle should expand to include Earth. Decades ago, the Gaia hypothesis (Lovelock 1972; Lovelock and Margulis, 1974) proposed that the living and non-living components of Earth make up a single organism and that there was some self-regulating process in place to support life. While this has always been a controversial theory and some scholars have dismissed it, others have begun to try to test the hypothesis (Lenton et al, 2018). They suggest that sequential selection – planets and their environmental conditions are affected by the life that is on them in either stabilising or destabilising states – explains the Gaia hypothesis (Lenton et al, 2018). They use the emergence of photosynthesis and the resulting increase in oxygen levels on Earth 2.3 billion years ago as an example (Dyke and Lenton, 2018). We are not suggesting that the Earth is wildlife, but we do think the Gaia hypothesis makes a critical point; all life is connected and all life, including the planet in its entirety, needs to be protected as best we can. In order for that protection to firmly take hold, we must try to end commodification in the form of property, end exploitation in wildlife industries, end violence against wildlife, give wildlife standing and rights, and combat speciesism, so that all species are visible and free from injustices. Wildlife criminology represents our first step in launching/extending this debate and in doing so sets out our attempt to discuss how harms (and crimes) against wildlife can be better addressed through criminological inquiry.

References

Agnew, D.J., Pearce, J., Pramod, G., Peatman, T., Watson, W., Beddington, J.R. and Pitcher, T.J. (2009) Estimating the worldwide extent of illegal fishing. *PLOS One* 4(2): 1–8 https://doi.org/10.1371/journal.pone.0004570

Agnew, R. (1998) The causes of animal abuse: a social psychological analysis. *Theoretical Criminology* 2(2): 177–209

Alamilla, J. (2018) The shifting legal landscape of bullfighting in Spain. LawInSport, 9 October. www.lawinsport.com/topics/articles/item/the-shifting-legal-landscape-of-bullfighting-in-spain#sdfootnote12sym

Alderman, L. (2014) Chefs fight for songbird. *New York Times*, 15 October. www.nytimes.com/2014/10/15/dining/the-ortolan-a-tiny-songbird-as-a-french-cause-celebre.html

Allan, J.R., Watson, J.E.M., Di Marco, M., O'Bryan, C.J., Possingham, H.P., Atkinson, S.C., and Venter, O. (2019) Hotspots of human impact on threatened terrestrial vertebrates. *PLOS Biology*. https://doi.org/10.1371/journal.pbio.3000158

ALRC (Animal Law Resource Center) (2014) Regulation of animal cruelty during rodeo events. www.animallaw.com/Model-Law-Rodeos.cfm

American Museum of Natural History (2010) Quantifying the relative abundance of juvenile Atlantic sturgeon, Acipenser oxyrhychus, in the Hudson River. [Learn & Teach] www.amnh.org/learn-teach/young-naturalist-awards/winning-essays/2010/quantifying-the-relative-abundance-of-juvenile-atlantic-sturgeon-acipenser-oxyrhychus-in-the-hudson-river

Anderson, R. (2019) Scientists are rethinking animal cognition. *The Atlantic*. www.theatlantic.com/magazine/archive/2019/03/what-the-crow-knows/580726/

Arkow, P. (1996) The relationship between animal abuse and other forms of family violence. *Family Violence & Sexual Assault Bulletin* 12(1–2): 29–34

Arlinghaus, R., Cooke, S, J., Schwab, A. and Cowx, I. (2007) Fish welfare: a challenge to the feelings-based approach, with implications for recreational fishing, *Fish and Fisheries* 8(1): 57–71

Arluke, A. (2006) *Just a dog: Understanding animal cruelty and ourselves.* Philadelphia, PA: Temple University Press

Arroyo-Quiroz, I. and Wyatt, T. (2019) Tráfico de vida silvestre entre la Unión Europea y México. *Critica Penal y Poder.* No 16

Ascione, F.R. (1993) Children who are cruel to animals: a review of research and implications for developmental psychopathology. *Anthrozoos* 4: 226–7

Ascione, F. (2009) Examining children's exposure to violence in the context of animal abuse. In A. Linzey (ed.) *The link between animal abuse and human violence*. Eastbourne: Sussex Academic Press, pp 106–15

Ascione, F.R. and Weber, C. (1995) *Battered Partner Shelter Survey (BPSS)*. Logan, UT: Utah State University

Avery, M. (2017) Grouse shooting: half a million reasons why time's up for this appalling 'sport'. *The Guardian*, 12 August. www.theguardian.com/commentisfree/2017/aug/12/grouse-shooting-glorious-twelfth-times-up-for-inglorious-victorian-sport

Baia, P.C., Guimaraes, D.A. and Le Pendu, Y. (2010) Non-legalized commerce in game meat in the Brazilian Amazon: a case study. *Revista de Biologia Tropical* 58: 1079–88

Baker, J. (1997) Trophy hunting as a sustainable use of wildlife resources in southern and eastern Africa. *Journal of Sustainable Tourism* 5: 306–21

Barry, B. (1989) *Theories of justice*. Hemel Hempstead: Harvester-Wheatsheaf

Bateson, P. and Bradshaw, E.L. (1997) Physiological effects of hunting red deer (Cervus cervus). *Proceedings of the Royal Society B: Biological Sciences* 264(1389): 1707–14. doi: 10.1098/rspb.1997.0237

BBC News (2017) Hare coursers 'becoming increasingly violent'. 6 January. www.bbc.co.uk/news/uk-england-lincolnshire-38530950

BCTF (Bushmeat Crisis Task Force) (2009) What is the bushmeat crisis? www.bushmeat.org/bushmeat_and_wildlife_trade/what_is_the_bushmeat_crisis [accessed 25 July 2012; link no longer exists]

Beetz, A.M. (2009) Empathy as an indicator of emotional development. In A. Linzey (ed.) *The link between animal abuse and human violence*, Eastbourne, UK: Sussex Academic Press, pp 63–74

Beirne, P. (2007) Animal rights, animal abuse and green criminology. In P. Beirne and N. South (eds) *Issues in green criminology*. Cullompton, UK: Willan, pp 55–83

Beirne, P. (2014) Theriocide: naming animal killing. *International Journal for Crime, Justice and Social Democracy* 3(2): 49–66

Beirne, P. (2018) *Murdering animals: Writings on theriocide, homicide and nonspeciesist criminology*. Palgrave Studies in Green Criminology. London: Palgrave Macmillan

Bell, L. (2001) Abusing children – abusing animals, *Journal of Social Work* 1(2): 223–4

Benton, T. (1998) Rights and justice on a shared planet: more rights or new relations? *Theoretical Criminology* 2: 149–75

Birch, J. (2017) Animal sentience and the precautionary principle. *Animal Sentience* 16(1): 1–16

BirdLife International (2017) *Emberiza hortulana* (amended version of 2016 assessment) The IUCN Red List of Threatened Species 2017: e.T22720916A111136121. http://dx.doi.org/10.2305/IUCN. UK.2017-1.RLTS.T22720916A111136121.en

Boat, B. (1995) The relationship between violence to children and violence to animals: an ignored link? *Journal of Interpersonal Violence* 10(4): 229–35

Bodkin, H. (2018) Black market betting fuels 'terrifying' surge in illegal hare coursing. *The Telegraph*, 24 March. www.telegraph.co.uk/news/2018/03/24/black-market-betting-fuels-terrifying-surge-illegal-hare-coursing/

Boesch, C., Crockford, C., Herbinger, I., Wittig, R., Moebius, Y. and Normand, E. (2008) Intergroup conflicts among chimpanzees in Taï National Park: lethal violence and the female perspective. *American Journal of Primatology* 70: 519–32

Borgerson, C., Rajaona, D., Razafindrapaoly, B., Rasolofoniaina, B.J.R., Kremen, C. and Golden, C.D. (2017) Links between food insecurity and the unsustainable hunting of wildlife in a UNESCO world heritage site in Madagascar. *The Lancet* 389: S3

Borrell, B. (2009) Some California amphibians may need a lift to survive climate change, *Scientific American*, 7 August. www.scientificamerican.com/article/california-amphibians-need-a-lift/

Bradshaw, G.A., Allan, N.S., Janine, L.B., Joyce, H.P. and Cynthia, J.M. (2005) Elephant breakdown. *Nature* 433(February): 807

Brantley, A.C. (2007) The use of animal cruelty evidence in dangerous assessments by law enforcement. Paper presented at the International Conference on the Relationship Between Animal Abuse and Human Violence, 18 September, Oxford Centre for Animal Ethics

BASC (British Association for Shooting and Conservation) (2011) *The taste of game: Game recipes.* Wrexham: BASC

Bronzi, P. and Rosenthal, H. (2014) Present and future sturgeon and caviar production and marketing: a global market overview. *Journal of Applied Ichthyology* 30: 1536–46. doi:10.1111/jai.12628

Brooks G., Aleem A., Button M. (2013) Fraud and corruption in horse racing. In G. Brooks, A. Aleem and M. Button (eds) *Fraud, corruption and sport.* London: Palgrave Macmillan, pp 108–21

Brosnan, S. (2011) An evolutionary perspective on morality. *Journal of Economic Behavior & Organization* 77: 23–30

Browne, A. (1993) Violence against women by male partners: prevalence, outcomes, and policy implications. *American Psychologist* 48: 1077–87

Brownmiller, S. (1975) *Against our will: Men, women, and rape.* New York: Simon & Schuster

Brymer, R.A. (1991) The emergence and maintenance of a deviant sub-culture: the case of hunting/poaching subculture. *Anthropologica* 33: 177–94

Burns, L., Edwards, V., Marsh, J., Soulsby, L. and Winter, M. (2000) Committee of Inquiry into Hunting with Dogs in England and Wales ['the Burns Inquiry']. London: The Stationery Office

Burkart, J.M., Fehr, E., Efferson, C. and Van Schaik, C.P. (2007) Other-regarding preferences in a non-human primate: common marmosets provision food altruistically. *Proceedings of the National Academy of Sciences of the United States of America* 104: 19762–6

Büscher, B., and Ramutsindela, M. (2016) Green violence: rhino poaching and the war to save Southern Africa's peace parks. *African Affairs* 115(458): 1–22, https://doi.org/10.1093/afraf/adv058

BVA (British Veterinary Association) (2012) *The Welfare of Wild Animals in Travelling Circuses (England) Regulations 2012: Unethical, ineffective and unenforceable.* www.bva.co.uk/uploadedFiles/Content/News,_campaigns_and_policies/Policies/Ethics_and_welfare/circuses_joint_briefing_on_draft_Regs_Oct2012.pdf

Calatrava, A. (2019) Argentine orangutan Sandra to head to US great ape sanctuary. Associated Press, 25 September. https://apnews.com/7019f1ed2eb04b27b96134a44ded4bdd

Cameron, G., Pendry, S., Allan, C. and Wu, J. (2004) *Traditional Asian medicine identification guide for law enforcers: Version II.* Cambridge, UK: Her Majesty's Customs and Excise and TRAFFIC International

Carmeli, Y.S. (1997) The sight of cruelty: the case of circus animal acts. *Visual Anthropology* 10(1): 1–15. doi: 10.1080/08949468.1997.9966717

Carmeli, Y.S. (2002) 'Cruelty to animals' and nostalgic totality: performance of a travelling circus in Britain. *International Journal of Sociology and Social Policy* 22 (11/12): 73–88. https://doi.org/10.1108/01443330210790201

Carter, H. (1999) Circus trainer guilty of cruelty to chimpanzee. *The Guardian*, 28 January. www.theguardian.com/uk/1999/jan/28/helencarter

Carter, T.J. (2004) Force against and by game wardens in citizen encounters. *Police Quarterly* 7(4): 489–508. https://doi.org/10.1177/1098611103253852

Challender, D., Waterman, C. and Baillie, J. (2014) *Scaling up pangolin conservation. IUCN SSC Pangolin Specialist Group conservation action plan.* London: Zoological Society of London. www.pangolinsg.org/files/2012/07/Scaling_up_pangolin_conservation_280714_v4.pdf

Chamovitz, D. (2013) *What a plant knows: A field guide to the senses of your garden – and beyond.* Oxford: Oneworld Publications

Chaves, W.A., Wilkie, D.S., Monroe, M.C. and Sieving, K.E. (2017) Market access and wild meat consumption in the central Amazon, Brazil. *Biological Conservation* 212(Part A): 240–8

Chaves, W.A., Valle, D.R., Monroe, M.C., Wilkie, D.S., Sieving, K.E. and Sadowsky, B. (2018) Changing wild meat consumption: an experiment in the central Amazon, Brazil. *Conservation Letters* 11(2). https://doi.org/10.1111/conl.12391

Chee, Y.E. and Wintle, B.A. (2010) Linking modelling, monitoring and management: an integrated approach to controlling overabundant wildlife. *Journal of Applied Ecology* 47: 1169–78

CITES (Convention on the International Trade in Endangered Species of Wild Fauna and Flora) (no date) What is CITES? www.cites.org/eng/disc/what.php

CITES (2016) The CITES species. https://cites.org/eng/disc/species.php

Clawson, E. (2009) Canaries in the mine: the priority of human welfare in animal abuse prosecution. In A. Linzey (ed.) *The link between animal abuse and human violence.* Eastbourne: Sussex Academic Press

Clements-Housser, K. (2017) *Over a million songbirds killed on Cyprus for a local delicacy.* www.earthtouchnews.com/environmental-crime/poaching/over-a-million-birds-killed-on-cyprus-for-local-delicacy/

Clubb, R. and Mason, G. (2003) Captivity effects on wide-ranging carnivores, *Nature* 425: 473–4

Clutton-Brock, T. (2009) Cooperation between non-kin in animal societies. *Nature* 462: 51–7

Cohn, P. and Linzey, A. (2009) Hunting as an abusive subculture. In A. Linzey (ed.) *The link between animal abuse and human violence.* Eastbourne: Sussex Academic Press, pp 317–28

Conboy-Hill, S. (2000) Animal abuse and interpersonal violence. Lincoln: The Companion Animal Behaviour Therapy Study Group

Consortium for Ocean Leadership (2019) The state of our ocean. https://oceanleadership.org/the-state-of-our-ocean/

Conway, W.G. (2010) Buying time for wild animals with zoos. *Zoo Biology* 30(1): 1–8

Cooke, S. and Sneddon, L. (2007) Animal welfare perspectives on recreational angling. *Applied Animal Behaviour Science* 104(3–4): 176–98

Corey, D. (2011) Equine welfare in the rodeo horse. In C. Wayne McIlwraith and Bernard E. Rollin (eds) *Equine welfare*. Chichester, UK: Wiley-Blackwell, pp 275–301

Dart, T. (2017) Bloodless bullfighting in Texas frontier country: 'I call it the ballet of life', *The Guardian*, 16 March. www.theguardian.com/world/2017/mar/16/bloodless-bullfighting-south-texas-ballet-of-life

Daugherty, P. (2005) Animal abusers may be warming up for more. Los Angeles Community Policing. www.lacp.org/2005-Articles-Main/LAPDsDedicatedAnimalCrueltyUnit.html

Davie, P.S. and Kopf, R.K. (2006) Physiology, behaviour and welfare of fish during recreational fishing and after release. *New Zealand Veterinary Journal* 54(4): 161–72. doi: 10.1080/00480169.2006.36690

de Bruyn, P.J.N., Tosh, C.A. and Bester, M.N. (2008) Sexual harassment of a king penguin by an Antarctic fur seal. *Journal of Ethology* 26: 295–7

Defra (Department for Environment, Food & Rural Affairs) (2012) Guidance on the Welfare of Wild Animals in Travelling Circuses (England) Regulations 2012. London: Defra

Defra (2019) Gove delivers legislation to ban wild animals in circuses. Press release, 1 May. www.gov.uk/government/news/gove-delivers-legislation-to-ban-wild-animals-in-circuses?fbclid=IwAR1WjvTE2mWteHhYglicA4CEhwbFw4CT9eJQucH_RWyubLTr3oBxBKQywCE

Derrida, J. (2002) The animal that therefore I am (more to follow). Trans. by David Wills. *Critical Inquiry* 28(2): 369–418.

Donaldson, S. and Kymlicka, W. (2011) *Zoopolis: A political theory of animal rights*. Oxford: Oxford University Press

Drury, R.C. (2009) Identifying and understanding consumers of wild animal products in Hanoi, Vietnam: implication for conservation management. [Doctoral thesis] University College London. https://discovery.ucl.ac.uk/id/eprint/16275/

Dubois, S., Fenwick, N., Ryan, E.A., Baker, L., Baker, S.E., Beausoleil, N.J., Carter, S., Cartwright, B., Costa, F., Draper, C., Griffin, J., Grogan, A., Howald, G., Jones, B., Littin, K.E., Lombard, A.T., Mellor, D.J., Ramp, D., Schuppli, C.A. and Fraser, D. (2017) International consensus principles for ethical wildlife control. *Conservation Biology* 31: 753–60

Dunn, S. (2002) *The social contract and the first and second discourses*. New Haven, CT: Yale University Press

Dyke, J. and Lenton, T. (2018) Scientists finally have an explanation for the 'Gaia puzzle'. *The Conversation*, 2 July. https://theconversation.com/scientists-finally-have-an-explanation-for-the-gaia-puzzle-99153

Early, R. and Fax, D. (2011) Analysis of climate paths reveals potential limitations on species range shifts. *Ecology Letters* 14(11): 1125–33

Edwards, A. and Gill, P. (2004) Introduction. In A. Edwards and P. Gill (eds) *Transnational organised crime: Perspectives on global security.* London: Taylor and Francis Group, pp 1–6

Elbert, T., Schaur, M., Moran, K. (2018) Two pedals drive the bicycle of violence: reactive and appetitive aggression. *Current Opinion in Psychology* 19: 135–8

Eliason, S.L. (2003) Illegal hunting and angling: the neutralization of wildlife law violations. *Society and Animals* 11(3): 225–43

Eliason, S.L. (2006) A dangerous job? An examination of violence against conservation officers. *The Police Journal* 79(4): 359–70. https://doi.org/10.1350/pojo.2006.79.4.359

Eliason, S.L. (2010) Death in the line of duty: game warden mortality in the United States, 1886–2009. *American Journal of Criminal Justice* 36: 319–26. doi:10.1007/s12103-010-9087-x

Eliason, S. L. (2016) Game warden perceptions of change in conservation law enforcement. *The Police Journal* 89(3): 218–26. https://doi.org/10.1177/0032258X16642450

Eliason, S., and Dodder, R.A. (1999) Techniques of neutralization used by deer poachers in the western United States: a research note. *Deviant Behavior* 20(3): 233–52. doi: 10.1080/016396299266489

Enticott, G. (2011) Techniques of neutralising wildlife crime in rural England and Wales, *Journal of Rural Studies* 27(2): 200–8

Epstein, B. (1997) The environmental justice/toxics movement: politics of race and gender. *Capitalism, Nature, Socialism* 8(3): 63–87

Farrelly, C. (2007) Justice in ideal theory: a refutation. *Political Studies* 55: 844–64

Favre, D. (2005) A new property status for animals: equitable self-ownership. In C. Sunstein and M. Nussbaum (eds) *Animal rights: Current debates and new directions.* Oxford: Oxford University Press, pp 234–50

Favre, D. (2010) Living property: a new status for animals within the legal system. *Marquette Law Review* 93: 1021–71

Felthous, A. and Kellert, S. (1987) Childhood cruelty to animals and later aggression against people: a review. *American Journal of Psychiatry* 144(6): 710–17

Fennel, D. (2008) *Ecotourism.* Abingdon: Routledge

Flack, J.C. and de Waal, F.B.M. (2000) Any animal whatever: Darwinian building blocks of morality in monkeys and apes. *Journal of Consciousness Studies* 7: 1–29

Flothmann, S., Kistowski, K., Dolan, E., Lee, E., Meere, F. and Album, G. (2010) Closing loopholes: getting illegal fishing under control. *Science* 328(5983): 1235–6

Flynn, C. (2002) Hunting and illegal violence against humans and other animals: exploring the relationship. *Society and Animals* 10(2)

Flynn, C.P. (2009) Women-battering, pet abuse and human-animal relationships. In A. Linzey (ed.) *The link between animal abuse and human violence*. Eastbourne: Sussex Academic Press, pp 116–25

Francione, G. (1995) *Animals, property and the law*. Philadelphia, PA: Temple University Press

Francione, G. (2000) *Introduction to animal rights: Your child or the dog*. Philadelphia, PA: Temple University Press

Francione G.L. (2007) *Animals, property and the law*. Philadelphia, PA: Temple University Press

Francione, G. (2008) *Animals as persons*. New York: Columbia University Press

Frasch, P.D. (2000) Addressing animal abuse: the complementary roles of religion, secular ethics, and the law. *Society and Animals* 8: 331–48

Galston, W. (1980) *Justice and the human good*. Chicago, IL: University of Chicago Press

Gamborg, C., Palmer, C. and Sandoe, P. (2012) Ethics of wildlife management and conservation: what should we try to protect? *Nature Education Knowledge* 3(10)

Garner, R. (2013) *A theory of justice for animals: Animal rights in a nonideal world*. Oxford: Oxford University Press

Gavitt, J.D. (1989) Unlawful commercialization of wildlife parts. *Transactions of the North American Wildlife and Natural Resources Conference* 54: 314–23

Georgiev, A.V., Klimczuk, A.C.E., Traficonte, D.M. and Maestripieri, D. (2013) When violence pays: a cost-benefit analysis of aggressive behavior in animals and humans. *Evolutionary Psychology* 11(3): 678–99

Gierstorfer, C. (2007) Primatology: peaceful primates, violent acts. *Nature* 447: 635–6

Gobush, K.S., Mutayoba, B.M. and Wasser, K.S. (2008) Long-term impacts of poaching on relatedness, stress physiology, and reproductive output of adult female African elephants. *Conservation Biology* 22(6): 1590–9

Godoy, R., Undurraga, E.A., Wilkie, D., Reyes-Garcia, V., Huanca, T., Leonard, W.R., McDade, T., Tanner, S., Vadez, V. and TAPS Bolivia Study Team (2010) The effect of wealth and real income on wildlife consumption among native Amazonians in Bolivia: estimates of annual trends with longitudinal household data (2002–2006). *Animal Conservation* 13: 265–74

Goldhawk, C., Bond, G., Gramdin, T. and Pajor, E. (2016) Behaviour of bucking bulls prior to rodeo performances and relation to rodeo and human activities. *Applied Animal Behaviour Science* 181: 63–9

Goodey, J. (1997) Masculinities, fear of crime and fearlessness. *The British Journal of Sociology* 37(3): 401–18

Grant, R. (2018) Do trees talk to each other? *Smithsonian Magazine* (March). www.smithsonianmag.com/science-nature/the-whispering-trees-180968084/

Groombridge, N. (1998) Masculinities and crimes against the environment. *Theoretical Criminology* 2(2): 249–67

The Guardian (2019) Orangutan Sandra granted personhood settles into new Florida home. 7 November. www.theguardian.com/world/2019/nov/07/sandra-orangutan-florida-argentina-buenos-aires

Gullone, E. (2012) *Animal cruelty, antisocial behaviour, and aggression: More than a link*, Basingstoke: Palgrave Macmillan

Haddad, W.A., Reisinger, R.R., Scott, T., Bester, M.N. and De Bruyn, P.J.N. (2015) Multiple occurrences of king penguin (Aptenodytes patagonicus) sexual harassment by Antarctic fur seals (Arctocephalus gazella). *Polar Biology* 38: 741–6

Hadidian, J. (2012) Taking the 'pest' out of pest control: humaneness and wildlife damage management. *Attitudes Toward Animals* 14: 7–11

Hall, D.L. (1992) Compliance: the mission of wildlife law enforcement. *Proceedings of the Annual Conference of the Southeastern Association of Fish and Wildlife Agencies* 46: 532–42

Hall, M. (2013) Victims of environmental harm. In R. Walters, D. Westerhuis and T. Wyatt (eds) *Emerging issues in green criminology: Exploring power, justice and harm.* Basingstoke: Palgrave Macmillan

Hargreaves, R. (2010) Countering the moral and ethical argument for canned hunting of captive bred lions in South Africa, *Journal of the WildCat Conservation Legal Aid Society* Summer (III): 7–26

Hawley, F. (1993) The moral and conceptual universe of cockfighters: symbolism and rationalization. *Society and Animals* 1(2): 159–68

Henry, B.C. (2004) The relationship between animal cruelty, delinquency, and attitudes toward the treatment of animals. *Society & Animals* 12(3): 185–207

Hillyard, P. and Tombs, S. (2007) From 'crime' to social harm. *Crime, Law and Social Change* 48(1): 9–25

Holmes, G. (2007) Protection, politics and protest: understanding resistance to conservation. *Conservation and Society* 5(2): 184–201

Honey, M. (2008) *Ecotourism and sustainable development: Who owns paradise?* Washington, DC: Island Press

Humphreys, J. and Smith, M.L.R. (2011) War and wildlife: the Clausewitz connection. *International Affairs* 87: 121–42. doi:10.1111/j.1468-2346.2011.00963.x

Humphreys, R. (2010) Game birds: the ethics of shooting birds for sport. *Sport, Ethics and Philosophy* 4(1): 52–65. doi: 10.1080/17511320903264198

Hutton, J.S. (1998) Animal abuse as a diagnostic approach in social work: a pilot study. In R. Lockwood and F. Ascione (eds) *Cruelty to animals and interpersonal violence: Readings in research and application.* West Lafayette, IN: Purdue University Press

Im, J. (2018) The illegal delicacy Axe ate on 'Billions' is a real thing – here's the story behind it. CNBC-Life, 6 May. www.cnbc.com/2018/05/04/real-story-about-the-illegal-ortolan-delicacy-eaten-on-billions.html

Intimate Ape, The (2015) Read the judge's decision that the orangutan Sandra is a 'non-human' person. [Blog, 25 October] http://intimateape.blogspot.com/2015/10/read-judges-decision-that-orangutan.html

Iossa, G., Soulsbury, C.D. and Harris, S. (2009) Are wild animals suited to a travelling circus life? *Animal Welfare* 18: 129–40

IPBES (Intergovernmental Science-Policy Platform on Biodiversity and Ecosystem Services) (2019) Global assessment summary for policymakers. www.ipbes.net/news/ipbes-global-assessment-summary-policymakers-pdf

Ireland, L. (2002) Canning canned hunts: using state and federal legislation to eliminate the unethical practice of canned hunting. *Animal Law* 8: 223–41

IUCN (International Union for the Conservation of Nature) (2015) *The IUCN Red List of Threatened Species 2015.* www.iucnredlist.org

IUCN (2016) *IUCN Red List categories and criteria.* http://s3.amazonaws.com/iucnredlist-newcms/staging/public/attachments/3097/redlist_cats_crit_en.pdf

IUDZG/CBSG (1993) *The world zoo conservation strategy: The role of zoos and aquaria of the world in global conservation.* Brookfield, IL: Chicago Zoological Society

Kaburu, S., Inoue, S. and Newton-Fisher, N.E. (2013) Death of the Alpha: within-community lethal violence among chimpanzees of the Mahale Mountains National Park. *American Journal of Primatology* 75(8): 789–97

Kalof, L. and Taylor, C. (2007) The discourse of dog fighting. *Humanity and Society* 31(4): 319–33

Kapner, S. (2019) Bans on fur threaten an industry's rebirth. *The Wall Street Journal*, 14 April. www.wsj.com/articles/bans-on-fur-threaten-an-industrys-rebirth-11555254000

Kheel, M. (1996) The killing game: an ecofeminist critique of hunting. *Journal of the Philosophy of Sport* 23(1): 30–44. doi: 10.1080/00948705.1996.9714529

Koshy, J.P. (2013) Rape in the animal kingdom. LiveMint, 15 January. www.livemint.com/Opinion/jkywrmQMip9SG6QVYDoe0H/Rape-in-the-animal-kingdom.html

Kymlicka, W. (2017) Animal law beyond the property/personhood impasse. *Dalhousie Law Journal* 40(1): 124–59

Laciny, A., Zettel, H., Kopchinskiy, A., Pretzer, C., Pal, A., Salim, K.A., Rahimi, M.J., Hoenigsberger, M., Lim, L., Jaitrong, W. and Druzhinina, I.S. (2018) *Colobopsis explodens* sp. n., model species for studies on 'exploding ants' (Hymenoptera, Formicidae), with biological notes and first illustrations of males of the *Colobopsis cylindrica* group. *ZooKeys* 751: 1–40

Lacy, R.C. (1995) Culling surplus animals for population management. In B. Norton, T. Maple and M. Nutchins (eds) *Ethics on the ark: Conservation and animal welfare*. Washington, DC: Smithsonian Press

Lasslett, K. (2010) Crime or social harm? A dialectical perspective. *Crime, Law and Social Change* 54(1): 1–19. doi.org/10.1007/s10611-010-9241-x

Lavorgna, A. (2014) Wildlife trafficking in the internet age. *Crime Science* 3(5). doi.org/10.1186/s40163-014-0005-2

Lea, J. and Young, J. (1993) *What is to be done about law & order?* (revised edn) London: Pluto Press

Leader-Williams, N., Bamford, A., Linkie, M., Mace, G., Smith, R.J., Stevenson, M., Walter, O., West, C. and Zimmerman, A. (2007) *Beyond the ark: Conservation biologists' views of the achievements of zoos in conservation*. London: Zoological Society of London

Lenton, T., Daines, S., Dyke, J., Nicholson, A., Wilkinson, D. and Williams, H. (2018) Selection for Gaia across multiple scales. *Trends in Ecology & Evolution* 33(8): 633–45

Levin, J. and Arluke, A. (2009) Reducing the link's false positive problem. In A. Linzey (ed.) *The link between animal abuse and human violence*. Eastbourne, UK: Sussex Academic Press

Lewchanin, S. and Zimmerman, E. (2000) *Clinical assessment of juvenile animal cruelty*. Brunswick, ME: Biddle Publishing Company/ Audenreed Press

Lindsey, P.A., Alexander, R., Frank, L.G., Mathieson, A. and Romañach, S.S. (2006) Potential of trophy hunting to create incentives for wildlife conservation in Africa where alternative wildlife-based land uses may not be viable. *Animal Conservation* 9: 283–91. doi:10.1111/j.1469-1795.2006.00034.x

Lindsey, P.A., Balme, G.A., Booth, V.R. and Midlane, N. (2012) The significance of African lions for the financial viability of trophy hunting and the maintenance of wild land. *PLOS One* 7(1). doi:10.1371/journal.pone.0029332

Lindsey, P.A., Balme, G., Becker, M., Begg, C., Bento, C., Bocchino, C., Dickman, A., Diggle, R.W., Eves, H., Henschel, P., Lewis, D., Marnewick, K., Mattheus, J., Weldon McNutt, J., McRobb, R., Midlane, N., Milanzi, J., Morley, R., and Zisadza-Gandiwa, P. (2013) The bushmeat trade in African savannas: impacts, drivers, and possible solutions. *Biological Conservation* 160: 80–96

Linzey, A. (2009) *The link between animal abuse and human violence*, Brighton, UK: Sussex University Press

Lovelock, J. (1972) Gaia as seen through the atmosphere. *Atmospheric Environment* 6(8): 579–80

Lovelock, J. and Margulis, L. (1974) Atmospheric homeostasis by and for the biosphere: the Gaia hypothesis. *Tellus* 26(2): 2–10

Lowe, Y., Bird, S. and Hayes, L. (2019) Campaigners accuse British zoo of animal cruelty for offering £15 tug of war with lion. *The Daily Telegraph*, 20 February. www.telegraph.co.uk/news/2019/02/20/ campaigners-accuse-british-zoo-animal-cruelty-offering-15-tug/

Lunstrum, E. (2014) Green militarization: anti-poaching efforts and the spatial contours of Kruger National Park. *Annals of the Association of American Geographers* 104(4): 816–32. doi: 10.1080/ 00045608.2014.912545

Lunstrum, E. (2015) Conservation meets militarisation in Kruger National Park: historical encounters and complex legacies. *Conservation and Society* 13(4): 356–69

Lynch, M. and Stretesky, P. (2014) *Exploring green criminology*. Farnham: Ashgate

Lynn, G. (2012) Cane rat meat 'sold to public' in Ridley Road Market. BBC News, 17 February. www.bbc.co.uk/news/uk-england-london-19622903

Mabele, M.B. (2016) Beyond forceful measures: Tanzania's 'war on poaching' needs diversified strategies more than militarised tactics. *Review of African Political Economy* 44: 153, 487–98. doi: 10.1080/03056244.2016.1271316

MacDonald, J.M. (1963) The threat to kill. *American Journal of Psychiatry* 120(2): 125–30

Mackie, J.L. (1981) Obligations to obey the law. *Virginia Law Review* 67(1): 143–58

Mann, K. (1992) Punitive civil sanctions: the middleground between criminal and civil law. *Yale Law Journal* 101: 1795–873

Marshall-Pescini, S., Dale, R., Quervel-Chaumette, M. and Range, F. (2016) Critical issues in experimental studies of prosociality in non-human species. *Animal Cognition* 19: 679–705

Mason, G. (1998) The physiology of the hunted deer. *Nature* 391(22). https://doi.org/10.1038/34045

Maxwell, S.L., Fuller, R.A., Brooks, T.M. and Watson, J.E.M. (2016) Biodiversity: the ravages of guns, nets and bulldozers. *Nature* 536: 143–5

McKie, R. (2012) 'Sexual depravity' of penguins that Antarctic scientist dared not reveal. *The Guardian*, 9 June. www.theguardian.com/world/2012/jun/09/sex-depravity-penguins-scott-antarctic

McPhedran, S. (2009) A review of the evidence for associations between empathy, violence, and animal cruelty. *Aggression and Violent Behavior* 14(1): 1–4

Mellor, D.J. (2016) Updating animal welfare thinking: moving beyond the 'five freedoms' towards 'a life worth living'. *Animals* 6(3): 21

Merz-Perez, L., Heide, K.M. and Silverman, I.J. (2001) Childhood cruelty to animals and subsequent violence against humans. *International Journal of Offender Therapy and Comparative Criminology* 45(5): 556–73. https://doi.org/10.1177/0306624X01455003

Messer, K.D. (2010) Protecting endangered species: when are shoot-on-sight policies the only viable option to stop poaching? *Ecological Economics* 69(12): 2334–40

Miller, D. (1999) *Principles of social justice.* Cambridge, MA: Harvard University Press

Milman, O. (2013) Australian scientists plan to relocate wildlife threatened by climate change. *The Guardian*, 17 October. www.theguardian.com/environment/2013/oct/17/australia-relocate-wildlife-climate-change

Milner-Gulland, E.J., Bennett, E.L. and SCB 2002 Annual Meeting Wild Meat Group (2003) Wild meat: the bigger picture. *Trends in Ecology and Evolution* 18(7): 351–7

Minder, R. (2016) Spanish court overturns a ban against bullfighting in Catalonia. *New York Times*, 20 October. www.nytimes.com/2016/10/21/world/europe/spain-bullfighting-ban-catalan.html

Minin, E., Leader-Williams, N., and Bradshaw, C. (2016) Banning trophy hunting will exacerbate biodiversity loss. *Trends in Ecology and Evolution* 31(2): 99–102

Mogomotsi, G. and Madigele, P.K. (2017) Live by the gun, die by the gun: Botswana's 'shoot-to-kill' policy as an anti-poaching strategy. *South African Crime Quarterly* 60: 51–9

Momii, M. (2002) A comparative study of wildlife law in the UK and Japan and the differences in cultural context. [Doctoral thesis] University of Kent

Monbiot, G. (2013) *Feral: Rewilding the land, sea and human life.* London: Penguin

Moore, A. (2005) Defining animals as crime victims. *Journal of Animal Law* 91–108

Morris, C. (1998) Justice, reasons and moral standing. In J. Coleman and C. Morris (eds) *Rational commitment and social justice.* Cambridge: Cambridge University Press, pp 186–207

Musing, L., Harris, L., Williams, A., Parry-Jones, R., Van Uhm, D. and Wyatt, T. (2019) *Corruption and wildlife crime: A focus on caviar trade.* Cambridge: TRAFFIC/WWF/U4 ACRC/Utrecht University/Northumbria University

Nasi, R., Brown, D., Wilkie, D., Bennett, E., Tutin, C., van Tol, G. and Christophersen, T. (2008) *Conservation and use of wildlife-based resources: The bushmeat crisis.* CBD Technical Series no. 33. Montreal/Bogor, Indonesia: Secretariat of the Convention on Biological Diversity/Center for International Forestry Research

Nurse, A. (no date) Dr Angus Nurse discusses legal personhood for animals. www.mdx.ac.uk/about-us/what-we-do/faculty-of-professional-and-social-sciences/school-of-law/features/dr-angus-nurse-legal-personhood-for-animals-is-still-some-way-off

Nurse, A. (2003) The nature of wildlife crime (enforcing wildlife crime in the UK), Faculty Working Paper No 9, Faculty of Law & Social Sciences, Birmingham: University of Central England

Nurse, A. (2009) Dealing with animal offenders. In A. Linzey (ed.) *The link between animal abuse and human violence.* Eastbourne: Sussex Academic Press

Nurse, A. (2011) Policing wildlife: perspectives on criminality in wildlife crime. Papers from the British Criminology Conference 11: 38–53

Nurse, A. (2012) Repainting the thin green line: the enforcement of UK wildlife law, *Internet Journal of Criminology* October: 1–20

Nurse, A. (2013) *Animal harm: Perspectives on why people harm and kill animals.* Farnham: Ashgate

Nurse, A. (2015) *Policing wildlife: Perspectives on the enforcement of wildlife legislation.* Basingstoke: Palgrave Macmillan

Nurse, A. (2016a) Animal abuse and domestic violence: exploring the link. *Journal of Animal Welfare Law* Summer: 1–5

Nurse, A. (2016b) Beyond the property debate: animal welfare as a public good. *Contemporary Justice Review* 19:2: 174–87

Nurse, A. (2017) Criminalising the right to hunt: European law perspectives on anti-hunting legislation. *Crime Law and Social Change* 67(4): 383–99. https://doi.org/10.1007/s10611-016-9669-8

Nurse, A. (2019) A question of sentience: Brexit, animal welfare and EU animal protection law. *Louisville Journal of Animal and Environmental and Law* 10(2): 32–59

Nurse, A. and Ryland, D. (2013) *Cats and the law: A research report for the Feline Advisory Bureau.* London/Lincoln: Middlesex University/ University of Lincoln

Nurse, A. and Ryland, D. (2014) 'Cats and the law: evolving protection for cats and owners'. *Journal of Animal Welfare Law* December: 1–6

Nussbaum, M. (2004) Beyond compassion and humanity: justice for nonhuman animals. In C. Sunstein and M. Nussbaum (eds) *Animal rights: Current debates and new directions.* Oxford: Oxford University Press: 299–320

Nussbaum, M. (2006) *Frontiers of justice: Disability, nationality, species membership.* Cambridge, MA: Harvard University Press

Odberg, F. (1992) Bullfighting and animal welfare. *Animal Welfare* 1: 3–12

Official Journal of the European Union (2012) Consolidated version of the Treaty on the Functioning of the European Union, 26 October. https://eur-lex.europa.eu/legal-content/EN/ TXT/?uri=celex%3A12012E%2FTXT

Olson, K.M. (2002) Detecting a common interpretive framework for impersonal violence: the homology in participants' rhetoric on sport hunting, 'hate crimes' and stranger rape. *Southern Communication Journal* 67(3): 215–44, doi: 10.1080/10417940209373233

Packer C., Kosmala M., Cooley H.S., Brink H., Pintea L., Garshelis D., Purchase, G., Strauss, M., Swanson, A., Balme, G., Hunter, L. and Nowell, K. (2009) Sport hunting, predator control and conservation of large carnivores. *PLOS One* 4(6). https://doi.org/10.1371/journal. pone.0005941

Pallotta, N. (2018) Though denied by New York Court of Appeals, habeas corpus claim for chimpanzees prompts reflection. Animal Legal Defense Fund, 7 September. https://aldf.org/article/though-denied-by-new-york-court-of-appeals-habeas-corpus-claim-for-chimpanzees-prompts-reflection/

Palmer, C.T. (1989) Rape in nonhuman animal species: definitions, evidence, and implications. *Journal of Sex Research* 26: 355–74

Pantel, S. and Anak, N.A. (2010) *A preliminary assessment of Sunda pangolin trade in Sabah*. Petaling Jaya, Malaysia: TRAFFIC

Parry, L., Barlow, J. and Pereira, H. (2014) Wildlife harvest and consumption in Amazonia's urbanized wilderness. *Conservation Letters* 7: 565–74

Patrick, P.G., Matthews, C.E., Ayers, D.F. and Tunnicliffe, S.D. (2007) Conservation and education: prominent themes in zoo mission statements. *The Journal of Environmental Education* 38(3): 53–60. doi: 10.3200/JOEE.38.3.53-60

Patten, R., Caudill, J.W., and Messer, S. (2014) The dirty South: exploratory research into game warden fatalities in the United States. In A. Nurse (ed.) *Critical perspectives on green criminology*. Nottingham: Flashmouse Publishing/*Internet Journal of Criminology*

Patterson-Kane, E.G. and Piper, H. (2009) Animal abuse as a sentinel for human violence: a critique. *Journal of Social Issues* 65: 589–614. doi:10.1111/j.1540-4560.2009.01615.x

Pemberton, S. (2016) *Harmful Societies: Understanding Social Harm*. Studies in Social Harm series. Bristol: Policy Press.

PETA (People for the Ethical Treatment of Animals) (2018) The leather industry. www.peta.org/issues/animals-used-for-clothing/leather-industry/

PETA (2019) We never gave up: PETA's triumph over Ringling Bros. www.peta.org/features/ringling/

Petrossian, G. (2015) Preventing illegal, unreported and unregulated (IUU) fishing: a situational approach. *Biological Conservation* 189: 39–48

Petrossian, G., Marteache, N. and Viollaz, J. (2014) Where do 'undocumented' fish land? An empirical assessment of port characteristics for IUU fishing. *European Journal on Criminal Policy and Research* 20(4): 1–17

Plant, M., van Schail, P., Gullone, E. and Flynn, C. (2016) 'It's a dog's life': culture, empathy, gender and domestic violence predict animal abuse in adolescents – implications for societal health. *Journal of Interpersonal Violence* 34(10): 2110–37

Pohja-Mykrä, M. and Kurki, S. (2014) Strong community support for illegal killing challenges wolf management. *European Journal of Wildlife Research* 60(5): 759–70

PRCA (Professional Rodeo Cowboys Association) (2019) *PRCA Livestock Rules.* www.animallaw.com/Model-Law-Rodeos.cfm

Preece, R. (1999) *Animals and nature: Culture, myths, cultural realities.* Vancouver: University of British Columbia

Radford, M. (2001) *Animal Welfare Law in Britain: Regulation and Responsibility.* Oxford: Oxford University Press

Rawls, J. (1971) *A theory of justice.* Oxford: Oxford University Press

Raz, J. (2016) The rule of law and its virtue. In R. Bellamy (ed.) *The rule of law and the separation of powers.* Abingdon: Routledge, pp 77–94

Regan, T. (1983) *The case for animal rights.* Berkeley, CA: University of California Press

Reid, N., McDonald, R.A. and Montgomery, W.I. (2007) Factors associated with hare mortality during coursing. *Animal Welfare* 16(4): 427–34

Reid, N., Magee, C. and Montgomery, W.I. (2010) Integrating field sports, hare population management and conservation. *Acta Theriologica* 55(1): 61–71. https://doi.org/10.4098/j.at.0001-7051.030.2009

Ripple, W.J., Wolf, C., Newsome, T.M., Betts, M.G., Ceballos, G., Courchamp, F., Hayward, M.W., Van Valkenburgh, B., Wallach, A.D. and Worm, B. (2019) Are we eating the world's megafauna to extinction? *Conservation Letters* 12(3)

Rollin, B.E. (2006) *Animal rights and human morality.* Amherst: Prometheus Books

Rook, D. (2011) The use of wild animals in circuses. *Web Journal of Current Legal Issues* (ISSN 1360-1326) 2011(4)

Rueppell, O., Hayworth, M.K. and Ross, N.P. (2010) Altruistic self-removal of health-compromised honey bee workers from their hive. *Journal of Evolutionary Biology* 23: 1538–46

Rytterstedt, E. (2016) 'I don't see myself as a criminal': motivation and neutralization of illegal hunting by Swedish Norrland hunters. In G.R. Potter, A. Nurse and M. Hall (eds) *The geography of environmental crime: Conservation, wildlife crime and environmental activism.* Basingstoke: Palgrave Macmillan, pp 217–39

Salvatori, V., Okarma, H., Ionescu, O., Dovhanych, Y., Find'o, S. and Boitani, L. (2002) Hunting legislation in the Carpathian Mountains: implications for the conservation and management of large carnivores. *Wildlife Biology* 8(1): 3–10

Saunders, T. (2001) *Baiting the trap: One man's battle to save our wildlife.* London: Simon & Schuster

Schaffner, J. (2011) *An introduction to animals and the law.* Basingstoke: Palgrave Macmillan

Schenck, M., Effa, E.N., Starkey, M., Wilkie, D., Abernethy, K., Telfer, P., Godoy, R. and Treves, A. (2006) Why people eat bushmeat: results from two-choice, taste tests in Gabon, Central Africa. *Human Ecology* 34: 433–45

Schleuter, S. (1999) Animal abuse and law enforcement. In F.R. Ascione and P. Arkow (eds) *Child abuse, domestic violence, and animal abuse: Linking the circles of compassion for prevention and intervention.* West Lafayette, IN: Purdue University Press, pp 316–27

Schmid. J. (1995) Keeping circus animals temporarily in paddocks – the effects on their behaviour, *Animals* 4: 87–101

Schneider, J. (2008) Reducing the illicit trade in endangered wildlife: the market reduction approach. *Journal of Contemporary Criminal Justice* 24(3): 274–95

Schneider, J. (2012) *Sold into extinction: The global trade in endangered species*, Santa Barbara, CA: Praeger

Schroeder, R. (2018) Moving targets: the 'canned' hunting of captive-bred lions in South Africa. *African Studies Review* 61(1): 8–32. doi: https://doi.org/10.1017/asr.2017.94

Schroepfer K.K., Rosati A.G., Chartrand T. and Hare B. (2011) Use of 'entertainment' chimpanzees in commercials distorts public perception regarding their conservation status. *PLoS ONE* 6(10). doi: 10.1371/journal.pone.0026048

Seymour, G. (2004) Animals and the law: towards a guardianship model. *Alternative Law Journal* 29(4): 183–7

Shani, A. and Pizam, A. (2008) Towards an ethical framework for animal-based attractions. *International Journal of Contemporary Hospitality Management* 20(6): 679–93. https://doi.org/10.1108/09596110810892236

Siebert, C. (2006) An elephant crackup? *New York Times Magazine*, 8 October.

Siegel, D. (2005) *Russische bizniz*. Amsterdam: Meulenhoff

Simmonds, M.P. (2006) Into the brains of whales. *Applied Animal Behaviour Science* 100: 103–16

Singer, P. ([1975] 1990) *Animal liberation*. [second edn] London: Cape

Singer, P. ([1981] 2011) *The expanding circle: Ethics, evolution and moral progress*. Princeton, NJ: Princeton University Press

Situ, Y. and Emmons, D. (2000) *Environmental crime: The criminal justice system's role in protecting the environment*. London: Sage

Slapper, G. and Kelly, D. (2012) *The English legal system*. Abingdon: Routledge

Smith, R. (2011) Investigating financial aspects of dog-fighting in the UK. *Journal of Financial Crime* 18(4): 336–46. https://doi.org/10.1108/13590791111173687

Sollund, R. (2019) *The crimes of wildlife trafficking: Issues of justice, legality and morality*. Abingdon: Routledge

Spira, C., Kirkby, A., Kujirakwinja, D. and Plumptre, A.J. (2019) The socio-economics of artisanal mining and bushmeat hunting around protected areas: Kahuzi–Biega National Park and Itombwe Nature Reserve, eastern Democratic Republic of Congo. *Oryx* 53(1): 136–44

Sweka, J.A., Mohler, J. and Millard, M.J. (2006) Relative abundance sampling of juvenile Atlantic sturgeon in the Hudson River. Final Report to the New York State Department of Environmental Conservation. NYUS Fish & Wildlife Service: Northeast Fishery Center

Sykes, G.M. and Matza, D. (1957) Techniques of neutralization: a theory of delinquency. *American Sociological Review* 22: 664–73

Tait, P. (2011) *Wild and dangerous performances: Animals, emotions, circus*. Basingstoke: Palgrave Macmillan

Tischler, J. (1977) Rights for nonhuman animals: a guardianship model for dogs and cats comments. *San Diego Law Review* 14: 484–506

TRAFFIC (2008) What's driving the wildlife trade? A review of expert opinion on economic and social drivers of the wildlife trade and trade control efforts in Cambodia, Indonesia, Lao PDR, and Vietnam. East Asia and Pacific Region Sustainable Development Discussion Paper. Washington, DC: World Bank

Trewavas, A. (2003) Aspects of plant intelligence. *Annals of Botany* 92(1): 1–20. https://doi.org/10.1093/aob/mcg101

Tribe, A. and Booth, R. (2003) Assessing the role of zoos in wildlife conservation. *Human Dimensions of Wildlife* 8(1): 65–74. doi: 10.1080/10871200390180163

Turner, N. (2000) Animal abuse and the link to domestic violence. *The Police Chief* 67: 28–30

Van Tuyl, C. (ed.) (2008) *Zoos and animal welfare*. Farmington Hills, MI: Greenhaven Press

van Uhm, D. (2016) *The illegal wildlife trade: Inside the world of poachers, smugglers and traders*. New York: Springer Nature.

van Uhm, D. and Siegel, D. (2016) The illegal trade in black caviar. *Trends in Organized Crime* 19: 67–87

Van Vliet, N. and Mbazza, P. (2011) Recognizing the multiple reasons for bushmeat consumption in urban areas: a necessary step toward the sustainable use of wildlife for food in Central Africa. *Human Dimensions of Wildlife* 16: 45–54

Vasquez, E.A., Loughnan, S., Gootjes-Dreesbach, E. and Weger, U. (2014) The animal in you: animalistic descriptions of a violent crime increase punishment of perpetrator. *Aggressive Behavior* 40: 337–44

Veasey, J.S., Waran, N.K. and Young, R.J. (1996) On comparing the behaviour of zoo housed animals with wild conspecifics as a welfare indicator, *Animal Welfare* 5: 13–24

von Essen, E., Hansen, H.P., Nordström Källström, H., Nils Peterson, M. and Peterson, T.R. (2014) Deconstructing the poaching phenomenon: a review of typologies for understanding illegal hunting. *The British Journal of Criminology* 54(4): 632–51. https://doi.org/10.1093/bjc/azu022

von Essen, E. and Allen, M. (2015) Reconsidering illegal hunting as a crime of dissent: implication for justice and deliberative uptake, *Criminal Law and Philosophy* 11(2): 213–28. doi 10.1007/s11572-014-9364-8

von Essen, E. and Nurse, A. (2017) Introduction. Special issue: Illegal hunting. *Crime Law and Social Change* 67(4): 377–82. https://doi.org/10.1007/s10611-016-9676-9

Watson, R.A., Cheung, W.W., Anticamara, J.A., Sumaila, R.U., Zeller, D. and Pauly, D. (2013) Global marine yield halved as fishing intensity redoubles. *Fish and Fisheries* 14: 493–503. doi:10.1111/j.1467-2979.

Wellsmith, M. (2011) Wildlife crime: the problems of enforcement. *European Journal on Criminal Policy and Research* 17(2): 125–48

Weston, B. and Bollier, D. (2013) *Green governance: Ecological survival, human rights and the law of the commons*. New York: Cambridge University Press

White, R. (2008) *Crimes against nature: Environmental criminology and ecological justice*. Cullompton: Willan Publishing

White, R. and Heckenberg, D. (2014) *Green criminology: An introduction to the study of environmental harm*. Abingdon: Routledge

Wickins-Dražilová, D. (2006) Zoo animal welfare. *Journal of Agricultural and Environmental Ethics* 19(1): 27–36. https://doi.org/10.1007/s10806-005-4380-2

Wilkes, D. (2012) Guilty of cruelty but not even fined: circus owner who let Anne the elephant be chained and beaten walks free. *The Daily Mail*, 21 December. www.dailymail.co.uk/news/article-2237469/Guilty-cruelty-fined-Circus-owner-let-Anne-elephant-chained-beaten-walks-free.html

Wilkie, D.S. and Godoy, R.A. (2001) Income and price elasticities of bushmeat demand in lowland Amerindian societies. *Conservation Biology* 15: 761–9

Wilkie, D.S., Starkey, M., Abernethy, K., Effa, E.N., Telfer, P. and Godoy, R. (2005) Role of prices and wealth in consumer demand for bushmeat in Gabon, central Africa. *Conservation Biology* 19: 268–74

Wilson, E.O. (2008) One giant leap: how insects achieved altruism and colonial life. *Bioscience* 58: 17–25

Wilson, E.O. (2016) *Half Earth: Our planet's fight for life*. New York: Liveright Publishing

Wilson, M., Wallauer, W. and Pusey, A. (2004) New cases of intergroup violence among chimpanzees in Gombe National Park, Tanzania. *International Journal of Primatology* 25: 523–49

Wilson, S., Anderson, L. and Knight. A. (2007) *The Conservation of Seals Act 1970: The case for review*. Scotland: Seal Forum.

Wise, S.M. (2000) *Rattling the cage: Towards legal rights for animals*. London: Profile Books

Wise, S. (2010) Legal personhood and the Nonhuman Rights Project. *Animal Law* 17: 1–12

Wise, S.M. (2013) Nonhuman rights to personhood. *Pace Environmental Law Review* 30(03): 1278–90

Wise, S. (2015) Update on the Sandra orangutan case in Argentina. [Blog, 6 March] www.nonhumanrights.org/blog/update-on-the-sandra-orangutan-case-in-argentina/

Wohlleben, P. (2016) *The hidden life of trees: What they feel, how they communicate – discoveries from a secret world*. Vancouver, BC: Greystone Books

World Animal Protection (no date) Ending the bear bile industry. www.worldanimalprotection.org/our-work/animals-wild/ending-bear-bile-industry

World Animal Protection (2016) Tiger selfies exposed: a portrait of Thailand's tiger entertainment industry. www.worldanimalprotection.org/sites/default/files/int_files/tiger_selfies_exposed_a_portrait_of_thailands_tiger_entertainment_industry.pdf

Wrangham, R.W. and Wilson, M.L. (2004) Collective violence: comparisons between youths and chimpanzees. *Annals of the New York Academy of Sciences* 1036: 233–56

Wright, J. and Hensley, C. (2003) From animal cruelty to serial murder: applying the graduation hypothesis. *International Journal of Offender Therapy and Comparative Criminology* 47(1): 71–88. https://doi.org/10.1177/0306624X02239276

WWF (World Wildlife Fund) (2017) Second-biggest direct threat to species after habitat destruction. http://wwf.panda.org/about_our_earth/species/problems/illegal_trade/

WWF (2018) *Living Planet Report – 2018: Aiming higher*. M. Grooten and R.E.A. Almond (eds). Gland, Switzerland: WWF

Wyatt, T. (2013a) *Wildlife trafficking: A deconstruction of the crime, the victims and the offenders*. Basingstoke, UK: Palgrave Macmillan

Wyatt, T. (2013b) The local context of wildlife trafficking: the Heathrow Animal Reception Centre. In D. Westerhuis, R. Walters and T. Wyatt (eds) *Emerging issues in green criminology: Exploring power, justice and harm*. Basingstoke, UK: Palgrave Macmillan: 108–26

Wyatt, T. (2014) Non-human animal abuse and wildlife trade: harm in the fur and falcon trades. *Society and Animals* 22(2): 194–210

Index